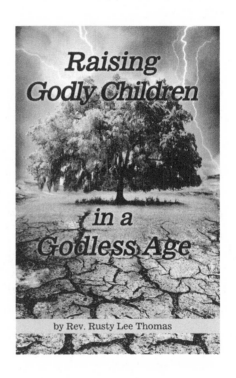

Raising Godly Children

in a Godless Age

by Rev. Rusty Lee Thomas

"As young boys growing up in Dallas, Texas, we cherished the moments Rusty Thomas spent in our home. While our parents were faithful to teach and live out the truths of Scripture, it wasn't until Rusty visited us that those truths began to take root even deeper. He affirmed the Bible's teaching and his message was filled with passion and fueled by compassion. What he spoke from God's Word and the way he spoke made so much sense to us. For every parent wanting to equip their children and engage them in God's destiny for their lives get this book, read it, and let it mark your home forever."

The Benham brothers,
David and Jason Benham

"Words can't describe how I feel about my father. He's been my rock and strong foundation. He's been with me since the beginning and has shown nothing but love and patience as we both navigated through these dangerous waters. He's been a perfect role model on what a proper Christian father, husband, minister, actor, and author should be. I just pray God uses me as much as He uses my father. I'm so honored to be called his son. He has always had the highest respect of those that are closest to him. He has my respect and love forever!"

Jeremiah Thomas
Summer of 2018

Raising Godly Children
in a Godless Age

by Rusty Lee Thomas

This book is dedicated to our son, Jeremiah Flip Thomas, whose brief life blazed like a shooting star reaching the world for Christ. Good night for now beautiful son. We will see you in the morning. For more information on Jeremiah's life, message, and charge to his generation go to:

www.jeremiahstrong.com

12/13/2001-8/26/2018

Raising Godly Children
in a Godless Age

By Rev. Rusty Lee Thomas

Table of Contents:

FOREWORD by Matthew Trewhella

In 1947, renowned sociologist Carle Zimmerman published his magnum opus Family and Civilization. He predicted that America would soon see divorce for any reason or no reason at all; that America would soon see legalized abortion; and that America would soon experience homosexuality run rampant. He said this in 1947 – nearly everyone found such assertions hard to believe.

Yet, no-fault divorce was introduced in the late 1960's which provided divorce for any reason or no reason at all. Abortion was declared "legal" in 1973 in the infamous Roe v. Wade opinion – and when it comes to rampant homosexuality, well… need I say more?

Zimmerman came to his conclusions by looking at the Greek and Roman Civilizations and other smaller people groups and societies.

Zimmerman concluded that the tipping point for when civilizations or societies begin to destroy themselves is when the people no longer want to have children. He states that he does not mean they want zero – but that couples want, at most, only one or two children.

He points out how from the time the Greeks didn't want to have children till they fell to the Romans was about 150 years. The time from when the Romans didn't want to have children till they fell to the Germanic hordes was nearly 400 years.

Zimmerman points out that the reason "not wanting children" is the tipping point where cultures begin their slide to destruction is because when men want to be husbands and fathers and women want to be wives and mothers – it produces in people virtue. But when men don't want to be husbands and fathers and women don't want to be wives and mothers – it produces within people vice.

America is committing familial suicide. America has been in a steep decline in the number of children couples are willing to have for over 150 years. In fact, we have quit replacing ourselves. The average couple now only has 1.8 children. Demographers point out that for a nation to simply replace itself, couples must have 2.1 children.

Civilization grows out of familism. In other words, family is the foundation of society.

Today in America, marriage and family are at a low ebb and in deep disarray. All the studies and statistics point to this fact. The attendant dire consequences are not needful to list here as everyone who lives in this culture sees it with their own eyes.

And this has been done by design.

The laws and policies of American governments – and all the West for that matter - are decidedly against families. A short perusal of divorce laws and procedures make this abundantly clear. No fault divorce, the decriminalization of adultery, and the legalization of homosexual marriage are all designed to demean and belittle marriage and family.

When one studies the history of these "laws," one sees that the people did not clamor for such changes, but rather that they were imposed upon the people by the state – most often through the federal judiciary.

Statism is the belief that nothing is beyond the state's reach. The state is the "be all" and "end all" within society. The state is looked to for the cure of every evil and the performance of every task. And every good statist knows that in order to strengthen the state, you must weaken the family. Family government has been attacked and invaded by civil government.

God has established four great governments, namely, 1). Family Government, 2). Church Government, 3). Civil Government, and 4). Self-Government. The first three governments are meant to develop self-government within the individual.

In a true federalism, all four great governments are important. In a statist hell, civil government invades the others and reigns supreme.

Atheistic societies tend to make the state God. They also tend to use the rights of the individual as a tool to invade every area of people's lives and weaken the other three governments – family, church, and self.

We now live in what some sociologists call an "atomistic" society – one in which the individual is held paramount. The desires, ambitions, and happiness of the individual take precedent over one's duty and responsibility to family.

Luxury and ease promote atomistic thinking. Luxury and ease convince people not to have children. The ill effects of luxury and ease are readily seen in a culture's sexual practices. Luxury and ease have proven historically to be an enemy of man.

Since the French Revolution, governments in the West have shown a propensity to promote and "legalize" sexual license. Governments have learned that the more sexually licentious a people become, the more easily they are controlled politically. A people preoccupied with their next quest to gratify themselves sexually is a people less interested in what their government is doing politically.

The people have no interest in freedom or liberty. In fact, the people have redefined freedom and liberty in their minds. Most Americans now think that freedom means you are free to practice whatever sexual perversion you like. The only freedom and liberty they are interested in is to make sure that their particular brand of sexual license stays "legal" and is not punished by the State.

Aldous Huxley, in his insightful work, Brave New World, also understood this about governments when he pointed out: "As political and economic freedom diminishes, sexual freedom tends compensatingly to increase."

And so it is in America. The statists have been busy making laws and policies to corrupt the morals of the citizens. We have a government that has been at war with Christ and the family for decades now.

Sadly, American Christianity has followed this demise. The first Christian body to ever accept birth control in 2000 years of Christian history just took place in 1930. Now all of Christendom accepts the use of birth control whether in word or practice – and most often in both.

American Christianity has also long bought into the lie of feminism and gender egalitarianism and is now busy rewriting 2000 years of biblical interpretation in order to accommodate itself to homosexual acts.

In other words, American Christianity has decided rather than confront the idols and thinking of the world it will confirm the idols and thinking of the world.

We live in the midst of a Christianity that is so drunk on the world's wealth and ease that the main function of most churches is to validate Christian's suburban lifestyles. American Christians love to listen to religious figures who suave their consciences and help them accommodate to the evil they embrace or tolerate in this world.

American Christianity helps the state affirm the secularization of America in the minds of Christians.

The two institutions in this culture that should be strengthening and affirming family – the church and the state – are not doing so. This means you are on your own. You must hold family dear. You must protect and cherish your familial relationships. You must sacrifice and show diligence to build your home and family.

The vast majority of present-day Christians are hell-bent to emulate the world, and in the end, immolate their God-

9

given purpose and created design. They're simply too busy following the world's preaching – pursuing wealth and ease – and having children hinders such goals. You must behave differently.

Rusty Thomas has given us a work that addresses family from both the presuppositional and practical levels. Thomas understands that, as Christians, we have children because we see God's created order declared in Scripture and we should obey it. We should live in fulfillment of it and not try to circumvent it.

We are to be a theologically-driven people. We must conduct our lives in accordance with Holy Scripture. We do what we do based upon what the Word of God declares. We have children, even large numbers of them, because we have fealty to the Lord and His Word. Our worldview is shaped by Holy Scripture.

God's Word makes it clear that God has a vastly different picture about children than the world does. God doesn't view children as a burden – He views them as a blessing. He wants us to have children, and when He gives us many, we are to take it as being blessed of God, not burdened or beaten down by Him. Blessed is the man whose quiver is full of them! (Psalm 127)

Phillip Longman is a well-respected, world-renowned, demographer. He's a secularist and a statist. He has written for the Council on Foreign Relations (CFR), an organization consisting of the cultural elitists of the world bent on implementing their statist social engineering plans through public policy. He was commissioned by the CFR to publish a paper addressing the plummeting birthrates in the industrialized and developing countries of the world. He had very sobering news for them, namely, people who are religious and who take their religion seriously are outbreeding them.

He concluded by stating, "As secular and libertarian ele-

10

ments in society fail to reproduce, people adhering to more traditional, patriarchal values inherit society by default."

Here's a pagan who gets it. Just by doing the demographics of the entire world – this is the conclusion he comes to – no society can survive without following patriarchal values, which he defines as a man and woman marrying, possessing defined complimentary roles, and having large numbers of children.

We now live in a nation where family has become the counter-revolution.

Martin Luther wrote in his day that "There are many who do not want to have children." The desire to prevent offspring is nothing new. Man has always, because of self-centeredness and the pursuit of materialism and ease, viewed having many children as a burden, and a detriment to self-fulfillment.

As Christians, we do not believe that our sons and daughters are a mere commodity that we can glibly pay someone $450.00 to exterminate, nor do we believe in birth control to prevent their conception. Rather, we view our children as precious because they are given to us by God. We do not view our children as products of random chance or as mere animals that evolved above the rest of the species, who exist simply for their own ends, designs, desires, and pleasures. Rather, we believe each of our sons and daughters were created according to the purpose of God in order to bring glory to Him and enjoy Him forever.

Most people have no understanding of family because they have embraced the hologram-family of American society. Rusty Thomas will give you the presuppositions for biblical thinking concerning family and he will give you practical application to build and strengthen your family in a wise and godly manner. He has lived it.

11

May Christ be praised in the earth!

Matthew Trewhella

St. Nicholas Day, 2018
Milwaukee, Wisconsin

*"I remember a great man coming into my house, at Waltham,
and seeing all my children standing in the order of their age
and stature, said, "These are they that make rich men poor."
But he straight received this answer, "Nay, my lord, these are
they that make a poor man rich; for there is not one of these
whom we would part with for all your wealth."*
Joseph Hall, English churchman, 1574 - 1656

Introduction

To be honest, if the basis for writing this book was due to my upbringing, it would just further the problems with the breakdown of the family, rather than providing Biblical solutions to redeem it. My family put the "unction" in dysfunction. My dad was a hardcore, Marine atheist. I was the first born son. The pressure was immense. You could not show weakness, fear, and God help you, if you shed a tear to relieve the pain of living a hellish, heathen life on the mean streets of Bridgeport, CT.

My dad was an alcoholic, womanizing, gambler. At times, he was extremely abusive. My mom was a complaining, bitter, hypochondriac, and an incessant chatterbox. Proverbs teaches that life and death is in the power of the tongue. We took a lashing every day (Proverbs 18:21). The same grumblings were drilled into our heads repeatedly with no relief. The more my dad abandoned his responsibilities to his wife and us kids, the more pain, loneliness, and the sense of abandonment afflicted my mother. Infidelity ran wild. And as they say in the military, "Crap rolls downhill" and my 2 siblings and I were on the bottom suffocating.

Out of 18 years of marriage, my parents separated several times. It was almost an annual event. There were times, literally, where my father had one arm and my mother had the other. As they bickered and quarreled, they were pulling me apart to determine who I was going to be with when they split.

I could remember the last separation before they divorced. They came to me confessing the only reason why they stayed together was for us kids. My profound response went something like this, "Are you kidding me? Do us all a favor and end this nightmare. You're killing us!" Apparently, they took my advice and divorced. Our family, like so many,

13

ended up on the ash heap of broken dreams, homes, lives, and marriages.

In God's mercy, He revealed Himself to me at 16 years of age. 16 was a banner year. Not only did my parent's divorce, but I quit school and left home to live on my own. Foolishly, I tried to make my way into this crazy world not really knowing how to survive. It was at 16 that I also came face to face with the living God. For brevity's sake, I'll spare you the powerful details of my conversion. Suffice it to say, just like the Apostle Paul, I got knocked off my high horse as God transformed my life. All the rage, perversion, profanity, drugs and alcohol abuse that had me bound was broken. They were driven out as God's truth and love filled my bankrupt soul.

The timing of God's salvation was impeccable. I had murder in my heart. I was filled with so much rage that I literally banged my head and face on brick walls screaming for release. When not afflicting myself, I looked for someone else I could beat up to pay for my torments and lack of relief from life's excruciating challenges. I was demonized. It was kill or be killed as far as I was concerned.

I was literally plotting the murder of my mother when God intervened. He saw me in my distress, heard my cries for deliverance, birthed me into His Kingdom and added me to His church. He not only saved my soul, He saved my mother's life.

Through a series of providential events, which may come to light later, (if I ever write my memoirs) I submitted to the call of God to be a preacher of His Word. As all typical young men, I also desired to be married. The problem was God knew that I was not ready to handle the responsibility of having a wife and children. In some areas of life, there were signs of maturity. In other areas, it would take marriage and having children to bring godly development.

From about age 22-28, I pleaded with God for a wife. I

might as well have prayed to the wall. It was as if God had his fingers in his ears shouting incoherent words to drown out my earnest longings.

I cried, pleaded, and applied every faith technique known to man trying to convince God to meet this need. I threw temper tantrums and threatened the heavens. Heaven's response: crickets. One day in utter desperation to the place of exhaustion, I collapsed on my knees. My earnest prayer went something like this, "I tried to convince you of my desperate need for a wife and the heavens are as brass and the ground as iron. It's like you don't even know me or care about me when it comes to this specific need. So, I'll tell you what. If you never grant my request for a wife, family or children, I'm still going to love you and obey you. For you are my God and I'm your son."

Two months later, I met my first wife. God got what He wanted from me and He granted what I needed from Him. This pattern of death that leads to resurrection would be a constant manifestation that would bring me to the next stage of service to our Lord through the years.

When I got married to my first wife, Liz, I thought my longings as a man had been resolved. Little did I know a reality check was coming that would soon rock my world. When we gave our vows, I fancied myself as a spiritual giant. Not long after, the unvarnished truth came to light. I was nothing more than a selfish, angry, lustful, emotionally immature brat that really had no clue what true love was or how to live it out faithfully towards God, my wife, or others.

When you are single, you have options. There is a lot of wiggle room when it comes to living out your faith. When you are married, however, options diminish. The black ink on the white pages of the Bible is no longer theoretical or abstract in nature. Christ must be the center and His Word must be applied or you risk losing everything you hold near

15

and dear in your life.

In my first year of marriage, my view of this holy union was very limited. The Scriptures said to marry or burn (1 Corinthians 7:9). I was burning and thought marriage was the solution. I simply wanted to have sex without sinning against God, my body, or others (1 Corinthians 6:18). Obviously, my revelation of marriage was tragically defective. By the way, do not be deceived, if you have a lust problem before marriage; be assured that marriage will not resolve it. It will only compound your dilemma with greater consequences if you do not repent and find Christ's deliverance from lust. There will be more on that topic later.

It was after our first year of marriage that we were compelled to exchange our limited view of marriage for God's view of marriage. It came in a very interesting way. God set us up and we were set up. Through a three-fold witness, God opened our eyes, broke our hearts, and birthed us into the battle to end the American holocaust called abortion. If you care to read that testimony, you can find it in the introduction to our book called Abortion Violation: America's Premier National Security Issue.

As we crossed the line of obedience to defend the lives of the preborn, we became convicted in other areas. Chief among them was God's view on marriage, family, and the blessing of having children. Here was the deal that confronted us. How could we fight and overcome abortion, when we were taking our marching orders for our reproductive practices from evil organizations like Planned Parenthood.

We were on birth control and had an anti-child worldview without even realizing it. We believed contrary to God's Word that this is what was expected of us as a young Christian couple. This mentality was passed down from our parents and we never took the time to hold up this view in the light of God's Word. We did not care enough to seek God's will concerning these primary issues of life.

Bottom line, the same reason why the world murders their children was the same reason why we did not want any children. Children were considered a burden, expensive, and a hindrance to our lifestyles. This was not only the mentality of the world, but we found to our dismay, it also ran rampant within the church who should know better.

When this hard truth came to light, deep soul searching commenced. Through brokenness, weeping, prayer, fasting, and much searching of the Scriptures, we repented. We immediately got off birth control. God turned the switch of life on and then broke it. My first wife and I had 10 children in 20 years. We literally raised our children on the frontline of the battle for the souls of men, the lives of children, and the future of our blood stained, perverted land.

On August 3rd, 2005, my first bride, Liz, went home to be with the Lord. She was 38 years old. Yet, she accomplished more in those years than most could accomplish in 3 lifetimes. Her heritage remains and continues to grow as our family presses on to the high call and prize.

To wake up a widower with 10 children to rear was a punch in the gut that almost knocked the life out of me. Life did not take a vacation because Liz died. The demands of our family increased and less help was available. There was hardly any time to grieve as some of my children were still babies. Though I tried desperately to get in contact with my feminine side, to everyone's shock, Daddy was not Mommy. Though I could possibly have remained single for the rest of my days, it was not good for my children to be without a mother.

It was there and then that I learned it is doubtless that God can greatly use a man that He has not deeply hurt. In fact, this poem by Barry McGuire became my faithful companion. McGuire wrote, "I walked a mile with pleasure and

17

she chattered all the way. But there was nothing I learned from pleasure when we walked along the way. I walked a mile with sorrow and nothing did sorrow say, but O the things I learned, when I walked with sorrow along the way."

My life and heart was plowed to its core. Thankfully, I had enough spiritual maturity to not shake my fists at the heavens and get mad at God. I had learned it was vain to ask why. We prayed for her healing and He answered. The answer was not what we wanted. He said no. My first wife, as all of our family, belongs to the Lord and He took her home to be with Him. Ultimately, she is far more His bride than she was ever mine.

One year later after Liz passed, God raised up another beautiful woman, Kendra, to take me on with 10 children. God truly brought beauty from ashes (Isaiah 61:3). She stepped in and God used her mightily to nurture our family back to health. She had twin daughters and that made 12 children. One year later, Kendra and I had our own daughter, Jubilee. We had her when I turned 50, so the name was appropriate. Altogether, we now have 13 children.

We have 6 children that are married and the grandkids are multiplying. 7 of our children have been shot out from the bow of family and church, and we still have 5 at home. We have one son, Jeremiah Thomas, who has passed on to glory. It is from this background and experience this book has been written. We pray the following lessons will prove beneficial to you the reader as you seek to raise godly children in a godless age.

IN KING JESUS' SERVICE,
Rev. Rusty Lee Thomas

Chapter One:
The Modern State of the Family

The American family has fallen upon hard times. There was a time in our nation when you could raise a family and neighbors, schools, churches, and government reinforced the values parents sought to instill in their offspring. Those days are long gone. Whatever support we once had from our culture, it has eroded away. In order for families to survive today, they need to recognize any aid we once knew, most of it, has turned to hostile opposition.

From public education, to feminism, to entertainment, to no-fault divorce, to birth control, to abortion, to homosexuality, to gender confusion, to government as savior welfare programs, the God ordained family has sustained blow after deadly blow. There seems to be just a mere semblance of family left in the home of the brave and the land of the free. Perhaps, the appearance is kept around as a museum piece to remind us of how backwards, unsophisticated, and unenlightened we once were as a nation.

This tragic scenario is not by accident, but by design. Just a cursory view of the Communist Manifesto, Humanist Manifesto 1 and 2, and Saul Alinksky's Rules for Radicals that he dedicated to the first rebel, Satan, will provide the narratives that reveal why families are in such disarray. In times past, faith, family, and freedom supplied the vital nutrients for a healthy national body. Foes within our national household understand the importance of this three legged stool that has sustained our nation. These virtues must be undermined and overthrown, if their godless agenda is to succeed.

Historically, sound families were viewed as a major building block to support healthy societies. Now, the God ordained institution of family is viewed as an archaic social construct that needs to be discarded or radically redefined.

The Anti-Christ powers that be, which believe in statism (government as god), understand that in order to amass power to regulate its citizens, they must weaken the family.

Sexual decadence has been one of the primary ways to undermine, faith, family, and freedom by those who seek tyrannical control over the masses. Chaos needs order and government by emergency provides both. This creates a perceived crisis, which manipulates us to give government more power to "solve the problem." Why waste a good crisis, especially, if it furthers the left's power base to create their secular utopia?

There is an old saying, "He who defines wins." What has our nation done to the Biblical and historical definition of marriage? How has our nation expanded the concepts of gender? Genesis reveals two sexes, "So God created man in His own image; in the image of God He created him; male and female He created them" (Genesis 1:27). Since the Creation, however, there are supposedly 56 distinct sexual, gender identities according to Facebook. Knowing the nature of lust, however, I'm sure they will add more and the perverted list will expand.

Sadly, this is part of the new orthodoxy of our times. If Christianity does not change with the times and embrace this godless confusion, the true church will be labeled heretical. If you study history, it never turns out well for those who are cast in the role of the heretic.

The feminization of the male combined with the masculinization of the female is the new norm. The majority of films promote women as the lead action figures. Commercials depict men caring for babies, cleaning the house, and washing the dishes, while high-powered women are taking care of business. This is part of the indoctrination that impacts the minds of unsuspecting Millennials.

Men are depicted as buffoons that need women to save

them from their idiocy and cowardice. Women are presented as aggressive, smart, assertive, and empowered. Men are superfluous and presented as mere fodder to feed the feminist war machine that rages against God, His divine order, and the specific gender roles He created for His glory and our good.

What has this rebellion done as America has dismissed the role of men as husbands and fathers? How has this impacted the role of women as wives and mothers? How has this affected our children? If we are accurate in our assessments, family in America has been weighed in the balance and we are found wanting (Daniel 5:27). Most families are out of divine order, spinning out of control, and heading towards the ash heap of history.

Modern social engineers view society as their grand laboratory. Citizens unwittingly become their guinea pigs. Through government edicts, public policies, and media lapdogs, Americans are being manipulated, programmed and conditioned. A massive campaign to desensitize us to evil has been successfully implemented. What was once considered unthinkable has now become main stream. In the midst of this collective brain washing, our duty as Christians is clear. We are not to be conformed to this world system, but to be transformed by the renewing of our minds (Romans 12:2). We are to be a separate, consecrated people set apart for the Lord (2 Corinthians 6:17).

America now stands on the sinking sand of Deconstructionism.

According to pbs.org, Deconstructionism is:

A term tied very closely to postmodernism, deconstructionism is a challenge to the attempt to establish any ultimate or secure meaning in a text. Basing itself in language analysis, it seeks to "deconstruct" the ideological biases (gender, racial, economic, political, cul-

21

ltural) and traditional assumptions that infect all histories, as well as philosophical and religious "truths." Deconstructionism is based on the premise that much of human history, in trying to understand, and then define, reality has led to various forms of domination - of nature, of people of color, of the poor, of homosexuals, etc. Like postmodernism, deconstructionism finds concrete experience more valid than abstract ideas and, therefore, refutes any attempts to produce a history, or a truth. In other words, the multiplicities and contingencies of human experience necessarily bring knowledge down to the local and specific level, and challenge the tendency to centralize power through the claims of an ultimate truth which must be accepted or obeyed by all.

In other words, Deconstructionism seeks to remove from the minds of men Biblical truth and historical lessons that define reality. The acceptance of post modernism and deconstructionism have conspired to help deconstruct the God ordained family. These aberrations also served to reinforce the lie of the garden.

If you recall, Satan attacked God's Law/Word, "Has God indeed said" (Genesis 3:1)? Doubt entered in and the enemy convinced mankind that we did not need God or His objective truth to govern our lives. Man was free to determine good and evil for himself. By this prerogative, man could become a law and a god unto himself. Our subjective impulses, thoughts, and feelings will now be the reliable guides to determine truth, reality, good, and evil. All philosophies, religions, and worldviews that deny the truth of Christ and His Word strengthen this stronghold.

From this faulty view of reality spring other worldviews that have conspired to deconstruct the God-ordained role of the family. Hedonism believes pleasure is the measure of all

22

things. Pleasure seeking therefore constitutes the ultimate meaning in life. The problem, of course, with this philosophy is that one man's pleasure may bring other men suffering. Besides, by what standard do we determine what is pleasurable and what is painful? For instance, should the pleasure of sexual immorality that leads to adultery trump fidelity to one's spouse?

Another worldview families must contend against is relativism. Relativism is a belief system that pervades much of our culture, government, schools, and sadly even some of our churches. Its premise is based on the fallacy that all ideas, philosophies, and religions are of equal value. According to relativism, there is nothing that is superior in knowledge, wisdom, and understanding and nothing inferior. All ideas are of equal value and all cultures have merit. So, if some cultures teach "love thy neighbor as thyself" and some cultures practice eating their neighbors, then who are we to judge the values and practices of others?

It is relativism that has led the charge to dismantle all sound judgment and erect the idol of tolerance that we must all bow before and pay homage. The homosexual agenda has used this idol to distort the "judge not" teaching of Scripture. This faulty interpretation not only served their agenda to gain acceptance, but it has expanded to supremacy. Islam and other sexual deviant practices are lined up to use the same playbook to implement their agendas as well.

There are other worldviews arrayed against the family. The last one I want to emphasize is called utilitarianism. This worldview thinks man's existence is based upon his usefulness. The utility of man removes his value as a human being made in the image of God. It replaces it with man as a "human doing."

A sign over one of the Concentration Camps in Nazi Germany, read, "Work makes you free." In other words, if

23

you cease to be useful in work, you must cease to exist. Extermination is the efficient means to deal with the failure to be useful. This mentality crushes love, compassion, and empathy towards our fellow man and if undetected, can subtly impact our relationships within the family.

Man's dignity must be safeguarded. This starts in the family. We are made in the image of God. Christ died to redeem His fallen creatures (Romans 5:8). It is these revelations, at least in times past, which inspired the church of the living God to defeat the ancient evils of infanticide, slavery, human sacrifice, and other atrocities. It should be our sincere prayer and righteous commitment that God reclaim the family and His church to once again end the evils savaging our generation.

All these philosophies and many others, such as, secular humanism, evolution, and atheism have helped to dismantle the family and bring chaos, confusion, and anarchy to negatively impact our age. The Scriptures warn, "Every man does what is right in his own eyes" (Judges 17:6). The honor due God, His laws, and will for mankind are spurned and denigrated with demonic glee. Good has become evil, and evil, good (Isaiah 5:20). Sins, which were once considered abominations, have been codified into "law." Tyranny is growing in our government at an accelerated pace as our culture turns liberty into licentiousness. Truly, those that hate God and His wisdom love death (Proverbs 8:36).

In light of these clear and present dangers, to be successful parents in the Kingdom of God today, you must also seek to be prophetic reformers. This means you must honestly assess the condition of marriage, family, and children, and take "what is" and give your life to make it what it "ought to be" according to God's design.

This is not for the faint of heart. It will take courage, humility, and perseverance. To establish a blessed family is not a hit or miss proposition. It certainly will not come by going along to get along. The path of least resistance makes both rivers and men crooked. It will take vision and a conscious effort. It will take mental, moral, and spiritual resources that must be faithfully applied. In the midst of the struggle, however, be reminded, "All things are possible with God" (Matthew 19:26).

Prayerfully, the following chapters will help equip you to meet these challenges and overcome them to raise godly children in this godless age.

Chapter Two: Parenting

"'Then she made a vow and said, 'O LORD of hosts, if You will indeed look on the affliction of Your maidservant and remember me, and not forget Your maidservant, but will give Your maidservant a male child, then I will give him to the LORD all the days of his life, and no razor shall come upon his head'" (1 Samuel 1:11). This was the prayer of Hannah

Most solid Evangelical churches make it a practice to dedicate newborns in their congregations to the Lord. Some reformed churches baptize their infants to welcome them into their covenant community. Regardless of the method, the desire is the same as Hannah. Genuine Christians are seeking to set apart their children unto the Lord. They want them to know Him and experience His great salvation at an early age. They want their children to love, serve, obey, and please the Lord all the days of their lives. They want their testimony to be not what the Lord delivered them out of, but what He has kept them from.

In a deeper sense, the most important persons being dedicated at a baby dedication to the Lord are the parents. They have the sober responsibility of raising their children in the fear and admonition of the Lord. In reality, they are setting themselves apart to train their children in the ways of the Lord, praying that when they are old, according to God's promise, they will not depart (Proverbs 22:6).

The word for train has an interesting connotation to it. Pulpit Commentary states, "The verb translated 'train' (chanak) means, first, 'to put something into the mouth,' 'to give to be tasted,' as nurses give to infants food which they have masticated in order to prepare it for their nurslings; thence it comes to signify 'to give elementary instruction,' 'to imbue,' 'to train.' The Hebrew literally is, Initiate a child in accordance with his way."

26

As Christian parents seeking to raise godly children in a godless age, we should be well aware of the external influences covered in the first chapter that will challenge our righteous goal. We must also be keenly aware of the internal struggle due to original sin. When a parent holds a cooing baby for the first time, it is a miraculous experience. The baby looks like an adorable little cherubim. Beneath the surface, however, is a child that was conceived in sin (Psalms 51:5). According to our fallen human nature, our children are born with a depraved bent. Like all mankind, we go astray from the womb (Psalms 58:3; Isaiah 53:6).

In the awesome adventure of raising 13 children, we never once had to teach, train, or instruct our children in the crafty arts of deception, lying, stealing, cheating, pouting, whining, pride, lust, selfishness, outbursts of anger, and fighting. These things just seem to have come with their birthday suits. It took a lot of effort, however, to oppose those sinful tendencies to help them overcome and adopt the fruits of the Sprit to form godly character.

It is through training children in the ways of righteousness and upholding God's standards in their life that prayerfully leads them to understand their great need for God's salvation. I can't tell you how many times my wife and I labored in prayer for the souls of our children. We homeschooled them, set up our family altar, read through the Bible every year as a family, prayed together, and diligently taught them God's Word. All the time, we would cry out to God to reveal Himself to them and confirm His truth to their souls.

It was one thing to teach them as parents, but it was an entirely different matter when the Spirit of the Living God confirmed His Word in their lives. At that point, the Christian faith went from theoretical in nature to a rock solid reality. Eventually, they all took ownership for the faith. We told them constantly that God does not have grandchildren. He

27

only has sons and daughters. They each must be born again to enter and see God's Kingdom (John 3:3).

As parents, we need to touch the palate of our children as it were in order for them to taste and see that the Lord is good (Psalm 34:8). They need to know that His word is truth. His ways are the best ways. His promises are sure. His wisdom, knowledge, and understanding are as high above men as the heavens are from the earth. He is trustworthy and just in all His dealings. The Judge of the earth always does what is right. He is not arbitrary, inconsistent, nor capricious. Therefore, we can rely on and have faith in God's holy and righteous character, word, will, and way.

Our holy calling as parents is to take these truths, chew on them in our own lives and touch the spiritual and moral palate of our children to create in them an appetite for the things of God. Our goal is to establish an inner monitoring system that points truth north and inspires our children to hunger and thirst for righteousness (Matthew 5:6).

Remember, these Kingdom realties do not come of their own accord. Children have to be trained to acquire them. Most children love desert and dislike what is good for their nutrition. Likewise, so it is with spiritual food and drink. As parents, whatever spiritual and moral diet we set before them, will determine to a great degree how their passions in life will be forged. Will unlawful lusts lead them astray or will their passions be properly channeled to produce good Kingdom fruit in and through their lives?

Notice as well, there is another important truth when it comes to training our children. Each child you are blessed with is a unique individual. They each have particular traits, talents, and skill sets. There are certain inclinations that we must be aware of to successfully ensure that when they are old, they will not depart.

This means we must investigate each child to ascertain

their strengths, weaknesses, interests, and inclinations to safeguard their strengths and shore up their weaknesses. If they have a particular God given gift, it is imperative that we help them hone that ability for the glory of God and the benefit of their future stations in life. It is clear from the parable of the talents that God expects a good return on any gifts he invests in the lives of men (Matthew 25:14-30).

For example, our family has two children with special gifts from God. My son, Micah, at four years old demonstrated a talent for art. His drawings at four went way beyond stick figures. In fact, his drawings were exceptional. We knew at that point we had a responsibility before God to make sure that gift was developed and set apart for God's glory and to be used to advance His Kingdom and great salvation in the earth.

One of our other sons, Josiah, at a young age stared at musicians leading worship at our church. Sometimes, I had to remind him to enter into worship and not just spectate. What I did not know at the time, he was studying all the musicians and seeing how they were playing their instruments. To our shock he came home, picked up instruments and began playing without a lesson. It took our breath away. Clearly, he had a gift from God. At 9 years old, he was a part of the worship team and could play all the instruments. As we homeschooled him, we took special care to develop his musical talent. He learned music composition, theory, and other related topics to develop his gift.

Developing children's gifts, talents, and natural skills to serve God is one of the chief ways for children to glorify God in the earth. Jesus is our example. The Father speaking of His Son's obedience and service unashamedly declared to the world, "This is My beloved Son, in whom I am well pleased" (Matthew 3:17). Every parent should live to say this of their children and every child should live to hear this from their

29

parents.

In His high priestly prayer, Jesus declared, "I have glorified You on the earth. I have finished the work which You have given Me to do" (John 17:4). Each of us, including our children, have a divine task set before us. When known, it answers all the deep philosophical questions, such as, who am I, why am I here, what is my purpose, etc. To disciple our children to know God through Jesus Christ our Lord is where they will find their identity, meaning, value, and purpose in life. To train them to faithfully live out that purpose ensures they will glorify God in the earth

Chapter Three:
The Doctrine of Children

As stated in the introduction, when my first wife and I got married, we were clueless to God's view on marriage, family, and the blessing of children. Through a series of life changing events, however, our views began to mercifully change. More and more, we became aligned with the revelation of God's Word concerning the importance of surrendering our reproductive life to the Lord.

Eventually, it dawned upon us that family planning really came down to a Lordship issue. When we first got married, we were dictating to the Lord how we were going to handle this aspect of our lives. If children did come up for our consideration, we decided for bookends. We wanted one son and one daughter. We foolishly assumed we had the power to create the sex of our children. Tragically, as science abandons Christian ethics, man's control over this and other realms increase. We thought that two children would make a nice, tidy, pristine family picture.

In essence, we were dictating to the Lord that he could be the Lord of other areas of our life, but when it came to having children, He need not confuse us with the truth. We had this covered. We knew better. We had modern technology and science to give us "wisdom" on family planning. The Lord could exercise His authority in some of the other rooms of our lives, but He need not inspect here. Instead of Him opening and closing the womb, we were more than capable of manipulating the womb to suit our chosen lifestyle.

Tragically, I dare say most Christians in America have similar views. Where did this view come from? It certainly does not proceed from Scripture. From Old to New Testament, there is a steady stream of godly evidence that the Lord encourages marriage between one man and one woman (It grieves me to have to make this distinction) and a quiver full of children to raise for His glory, dominion, and salvation in the earth.

For the rest of this chapter, we will go on a little journey together to get the mind of the Lord on His view of children. A good place to start is at the beginning. It is there we discover the Cultural Mandate:

> So God created man in His own image; in the image of God He created him; male and female He created them. Then God blessed them, and God said to them, "Be fruitful and multiply; fill the earth and subdue it; have dominion over the fish of the sea, over the birds of the air, and over every living thing that moves on the earth" (Genesis 1:27, 28).

Notice there is a direct connection between being fruitful/multiply and subdue/dominion. Amazingly, this mandate continued after the Fall. God reiterated this covenant command to Noah after the flood (Genesis 8:17, 9:1) It therefore remains the modus operandi of the Lord. Even though sin entered the earth along with the subsequent consequences of death, hell, and the grave, yet God still calls mankind to be fruitful and multiply. He has never wavered on this aspect of His will for His fallen creatures.

We see the benefit of this mandate demonstrated through the descendants of Hannah. Heman was the grandson of Samuel the prophet, great-grandson of Hannah. Heman "was the first of the three Levites to whom was committed the vocal and instrumental music of the temple service in the reign of David." According to the International Standard Bible Encyclopedia, "Heman seems also to have been a man of spiritual power" because he is called "'the king's seer in matters of God'." We read in 1 Chronicles 25:5, "All these were the sons of Heman the king's seer, according to the promise of God to exalt him, for God had given Heman fourteen sons and three daughters" (English Standard Version).

The New Living Translation reads, "All these were the sons of Heman, the king's seer, for God had honored him with fourteen sons and three daughters."

The same passage in the Wycliffe Bible states, "All these, the sons of Heman were prophets of the king in the words of God, that he should enhance the horn, or strength. And God gave to Heman fourteen sons and three daughters.

Interestingly, Heman's father was Joel, the firstborn of Samuel. Matthew Henry wrote in his commentary on the Bible, "Samuel had given his sons so good an education, and they had given him such good hopes of their doing well, and gained such a reputation in Israel, that he made them judges, assistants to him awhile, and afterwards deputies under him at Beersheeba." Yet Joel and his brother Abijah "did not walk in his ways, but turned aside after dishonest gain and took bribes and perverted justice" (New American Standard Bible).

Although Joel did not execute justice, the blessings of obedience found in Deuteronomy 28:4 rested on his child, Heman. Heman means faithful. This faithful man, grandson of Samuel and great-grandson of Hannah, was blessed with seventeen children to rear in the fear and admonition of the Lord. God was honoring Heman with each new child. The children were gifts from God to increase his power and influence. God advanced his kingdom through Heman and his posterity. So far did Heman's influence reach in the annals of history, two of his descendants were part of the great reformation in the time of King Hezekiah.

According to Deuteronomy 28:4, prosperity, wealth, and blessing included the "fruit of thy body." Today, we would

Smith's Bible Dictionary, s.v. "Heman"
International Standard Bible Encyclopedia, 1915, s.v. "Heman"

consider this teaching heretical. Modern man consumed by pleasure seeking and selfish materialism rejects this aspect of Biblical fruitfulness.

The Matriarchs of old, however, believed in having children. They longed for lots of them. In fact, they believed a barren womb was part of the curse. The distraught pain experienced by Hannah as she lamented her barren womb before God reveals the deep longing of motherhood back in the day. She was desperate to have children. Her intense prayer, which flowed from the bitterness of her soul, was initially misinterpreted by the High Priest, Eli. He mistakenly thought she was a drunken, mad, woman. Though Eli's discernment level did not rise to the occasion, thankfully the Lord still hearkened to Hannah and graciously opened her womb.

The Matriarch, Rachel, also felt the gnawing sensation of a barren womb. She cried to Jacob, "Give me children or else I die" (Genesis 30:1)! Most would probably consider her desire for children to be a bit extreme. Biblically, however, she carried the sentiment of that era. We have come a long way baby since this motherly impulse was lived out by faithful women of old. Today, feminism has all but destroyed this maternal aspiration. As a result, most believe the barren womb is the blessing and the fruitful womb, the curse.

The Blessing of Abraham

"Blessing I will bless you, and multiplying I will multiply your descendants as the stars of the heaven and as the sand which is on the seashore; and your descendants shall possess the gate of their enemies. In your seed all the nations of the earth shall be blessed, because you have obeyed My voice" (Genesis 22:17, 18).

I've heard many sermons on Abraham's blessing, but most

34

preachers were strangely silent on a few crucial aspects. They emphasized the promises of wealth, influence, and expansion, but seem to reject the means to its fulfillment. It takes descendants. It takes seed. It takes children that will rise up to possess the gates of their enemies.

Gates in the Old Testament represented the three fold seat of authority. Gates referred to the seat of political authority, the seat of judicial authority, and the seat of commerce (Deuteronomy 16:18–19, 17:5; 1 Kings 22:10; 2 Kings 7:1). The saints of old prized this aspect of the blessing of Abraham. Case in point, once Rebekah submitted to becoming Isaac's bride, Abraham's servants pronounced this blessing upon her. Genesis 24:60 records, "And they blessed Rebekah, and said unto her, Thou art our sister, be thou the mother of thousands of millions, and let thy seed possess the gate of those which hate them."

The Psalmist would add a hearty amen to this blessing. Psalms 127:3-5 states, "Behold, children are a heritage from the LORD, the fruit of the womb is a reward. Like arrows in the hand of a warrior, so are the children of one's youth. Happy is the man who has his quiver full of them; they shall not be ashamed, but shall speak with their enemies in the gate."

It was this Scripture that renewed my mind the most when it came to the crucial topic of children. Let's proceed to unpack this vital passage. First, children are a heritage; the fruit of the womb is a reward. How many Christians believe this statement today? Do most view children as blessings or burdens? Are they regrets or rewards? Does God bring children into our lives as an encumbrance or to provide an inheritance? Are they too expensive or are they Kingdom ammunition? With all our clamoring for God's blessings as Christians, do we desire these gifts, rewards, and heritage? If not, why not?

Secondly, God relates children to arrows. How many

35

would make a similar comparison? Yet, in God's Kingdom it makes perfect sense. It denotes that we are in a war, a global battle that is raging for the souls of men, the lives of children, and the future of our poor fallen world. Clearly, God views children as Kingdom ammunition. He desires a godly seed to fill the earth (Malachi 2:15).

In Genesis, we discover Satan instigated this cosmic conflict, but Almighty God declared war. Genesis 3:15 reveals the nature of this battle. God's Word states, "And I will put enmity between you and the woman, and between your seed and her Seed; He shall bruise your head, and you shall bruise His heel."

This is the first passage that mentions the promise of the Gospel of the Kingdom. It reveals God will raise up a Mighty Champion and a Great Deliverer who will suffer a bruised heel (Crucifixion) and crush Satan's head in the process. Notice as well, this hostility was not confined to just the Messiah and Satan. There is another element involved. It is also a battle between two seeds, the seed of the Woman and the seed of the serpent.

God promised the world that through Abraham and His seed, singular, He was going to bless all the families and nations of the world (Genesis 12:3, 22:18). The Apostle Paul in the New Testament pinpoints the singular Seed. Galatians 3:16 states, "Now to Abraham and his Seed were the promises made. He does not say, "And to seeds," as of many, but as of one, "And to your Seed," who is Christ."

In the Old Testament, God split up mankind into two categories, Jew and Gentile. At the first advent of Jesus Christ, the designation changed. The two categories today are "in Adam" or "in Christ." If a person is in Adam, he is dead in his trespasses and sins. If a person is in Christ, he is alive to God and dead to sin. There are more examples, such as, the righteous and the wicked. Regardless, these designations reveal

36

the battle between the two seeds.

In this battle, God has determined that the Seed of the Woman, which is fulfilled in Jesus Christ, will eventually emerge victorious in time and history. It is this seed that came through Abraham that God has promised to bless all the families and the nations of the earth.

Though, we all start in life as a part of the seed of the serpent, through the seed of God's Word, we are born again and transferred from the powers of darkness (The seed of the serpent realm) and safely placed in the Kingdom of God's dear Son of His love (The seed of the Woman realm) (1 Peter 1:23; Colossians 1:13).

If we, as God's people, pray "thy Kingdom come and thy will be done on earth as it is in heaven," then in time and history, we must live our lives to see it come to pass in Jesus' name (Matthew 6:10)! Obviously, one of the main ways this takes place is through evangelism. The faithful proclamation and modeling of the Gospel of the Kingdom is crucial to reach those who are lost in sin. They must be convicted to surrender their lives to the Lordship of Christ for the redemption of their souls.

Besides that, however, getting married to a godly spouse and walking in fidelity towards God and each other helps spread this vision and mission. After establishing this godly foundation, submitting to the Lord your reproductive life and trusting Him to open or close the womb plays a significant role as well.

When Jesus spoke of children in the New Testament, He strongly connected children to His Kingdom. Matthew 18:1–6 reveals:

> At that time the disciples came to Jesus, saying, "Who then is greatest in the kingdom of heaven?" Then Jesus called a little child to Him, set him in the midst of them, and said, "Assuredly, I say to you, unless you are

converted and become as little children, you will by no means enter the kingdom of heaven. Therefore whoever humbles himself as this little child is the greatest in the kingdom of heaven. Whoever receives one little child like this in My name receives Me.

In context, the apostles were competing over who was to be greatest in the kingdom of God. In the midst of their carnal outburst, Jesus placed a child before them. He used the child as an object lesson so that they might understand more clearly the fundamental nature of his kingdom. Jesus called the child, and the child obeyed by coming to him. In essence, Jesus taught that except a person has childlike faith and a humble heart, he cannot enter God's kingdom.

In another passage, Jesus made a more startling comparison between children and the Kingdom. Matthew 19:13–15 states:

Then were there brought unto him little children, that he should put his hands on them, and pray: and the disciples rebuked them. But Jesus said, Suffer little children, and forbid them not, to come unto me: for of such is the kingdom of heaven. And he laid his hands on them, and departed thence.

God's Word describes parents bringing their little children to Jesus to bless them. Instead of the disciples welcoming the opportunity, they rebuked the parents and tried to send the children away. Jesus stopped the madness and declared, "Let the little children come to Me, and do not forbid them: for such is the kingdom of heaven." The implications of this passage of Scripture are colossal. It gets to the heart of how children are an integral part the Kingdom of God. One cannot escape the incredible equation put forth by our Lord. In his divine mind, children equal the Kingdom of God.

Do we love the Lord? Does our love for Him translate to obedience to His commands (John 14:15, 21) Do we want to see the Gospel go forth and God's Kingdom advance? Do we desire all of God's blessings, including children? Do we understand the significance of children and their important role to see all this come to pass in Jesus' name?

In order to raise godly children in a godless age, it is vital that we reject the anti-child mentality that afflicts our age and even the church. We must return to understand that one of God's ways to redeem a godless age is by Christians having and raising godly children. We need godly parents who will take the time to train their offspring and then shoot them out from the bow of family and church to possess the gates of their enemies as God promised.

Chapter Four: Education

"I am very much afraid that schools will prove to be the great gates of hell unless they diligently labor in explaining the Scriptures, engraving them in the hearts of youth. I advise no one to place his child where the Scriptures do not reign paramount. Every institution in which men are not increasingly occupied with the Word of God must become corrupt." –Martin Luther

After we settle the issue that children are God's gifts and that He desires families to fill the earth with godly seed, we also have to determine that we will be good stewards of these precious gifts. This means we must seriously consider the Biblical model for educating our young. To miss this vital aspect is to fail in raising godly children in a godless age.

Without question, government sponsored public education is one of the main culprits that have served to destroy the Christian faith amongst our young. Depending on different sources and studies, somewhere from 80 to 85 percent of Christian young who are reared in Christian homes and attended Christian churches defect from the faith by their first year in college. Some do indeed recover and return as prodigals, while most remain shipwrecked in life (1 Timothy 1:19).

John Dunphy, in the Humanist Magazine from 1983 revealed the diabolical agenda:

> I am convinced that the battle for humankind's future must be waged and won in the public school classroom by teachers who correctly perceive their roles as the proselytizers of a new faith: a religion of humanity that recognizes and respects the spark of what theologians call divinity in every human being. These teachers must embody the same selfless dedication as the most rabid fundamentalist preachers, for they will be ministers of another sort, utilizing a classroom in-

instead of a pulpit to convey humanist values in whatever they teach, regardless of the educational level – preschool, day care, or large state university. The classroom must and will become an arena of conflict between the old and the new – the rotting corpse of Christianity, together with all its adjacent evils and misery, and the new faith of Humanism, resplendent in its promise of a world in which the never-realized Christian ideal of love thy neighbor will finally be achieved.

To this day, we may have a lot of young people filling our pews. They participate in church youth group activities, and yet, they still walk in lockstep with the spirit of the age and are addicted to the idols of their peers. Their bodies may be present, but their hearts and minds belong to another. Tragically, their hearts are far from God and distant from their parents as they bond, in most cases, with their pagan teachers and friends at school.

King Solomon in the God inspired book of wisdom, Proverbs, gave this instruction. He spoke it as a king/father attempting to disciple his children. The godly goal was to pass the scepter of righteousness, which establishes a multi-generational Kingdom vision to the next generation. He stated, "My son, give me your heart, and let your eyes observe my ways" (Proverbs 23:26, ESV)

In the midst of life's challenges and struggles, God desires to establish a safe haven for our children's hearts. Obviously, first and foremost, the greatest refuge of their hearts is discovered in the Lord, Himself. God Word promises, "The name of the LORD is a strong tower, the righteous run to it and are safe" (Proverbs 18:10). Besides this, however, it is incumbent upon the father to safeguard the hearts of his children. He is not just there to provide the essentials of life or to protect their bodies from physical harm. He is also responsible to provide a resting place for the hearts of his children who are prone to wander.

In today's world filled with business, activities, and addictions to modern technology, (phones, computers, entertainment, video games and such) tragically, it is the father that spends the least amount of time with his children. This discrepancy has far reaching implications.

This may come as a shock. The majority, if not all Scriptural admonishments, concerning the rearing of children is addressed to the fathers. There is never a time in the Bible where God calls disadvantaged children the motherless, the stateless, or the churchless. It is always the fatherless.

The consequence of disconnection between a father and his children in the modern era is overwhelming. Look at any data that reveals the brokenness of our nation and ultimately, you can trace most of it back to some form of fatherlessness.

This is true whether the father abandoned his children physically or not. If there is not a conscientious attempt by fathers to connect spiritually, emotionally, and mentally with their children, the children will suffer the wound of father hunger. This means our girls will be tempted to search for love in all the wrong places. Every Tom, Dick, and Harry will be more than willing to exploit our daughters. Our boys will be tempted to be either a narcissist, macho bully or a feminized male struggling with his masculine identity.

God warned that the sins of the fathers could reach to the third and fourth generation to those who hate Him (Exodus 20:5). Again, it is not the sins of the mother, the sins of the church, nor the sins of the state. It is the godly influence of the father or the lack thereof that will have dramatic impact upon their children's future. What fathers say or do not say, do or do not do, will impact future generations. Fatherhood is serious Kingdom business. It demonstrates the high and lofty position that most men ignore, reject, abandon, or by God's grace, embrace. If you are a father reading this, I pray you are the latter.

Secondarily, Solomon wanted his children to observe his ways. He desired his children to see how he conducted his private and public affairs and take note how he handled his duty as a man in his religious life, family life, and his vocation as king. He knew it was critical to leave a faithful pattern for his children to emulate in life.

The Apostle Paul, picking up on this theme in the New Testament, taught elders, "Likewise, exhort the young men to be sober-minded, in all things showing yourself to be a pattern of good works; in doctrine showing integrity, reverence, incorruptibility, sound speech that cannot be condemned, that one who is an opponent may be ashamed, having nothing evil to say of you" (Titus 2:6-8). He said of himself (Paul), "Follow me as I follow Christ" (1 Corinthians 11:1).

There is a story from the life of General Robert E. Lee that serves as a good example to highlight these responsibilities that come with fatherhood. Apparently, General Lee was strolling in the snow discussing with a subordinate the plight of the war effort. At some point in the discussion, the lower ranked soldier looked behind them and noticed the General's son following in his father's footsteps. The boy was placing his little feet in the larger foot prints left by his Dad. When the soldier alerted General Lee to the devotion of his son following in his footsteps, General Lee responded, "Then I better walk straight, strong, and true."

The hearty pilgrims that landed at Plymouth Rock desired the same legacy. William Bradford in his Plymouth Plantation wrote, "Lastly, (and which was not the least), a great hope and inward zeal they had of laying some good foundation, or at least to make some way thereunto, for the propagating and advancing of the kingdom of Christ in those

43

remote parts of the world; yea, though they should be but even as stepping-stones unto others for the performing of so great a work."

There is a Christian song that sums up the heartfelt commitment of those courageous souls who went before us to carve out the Kingdom of God upon our shores. It is called, "May All Who Come behind Us Find Us Faithful." The words capture the essence of what fathers and mothers should desire to pass on to their children, "Let those who come behind us find us faithful, may the fire of our devotion light their way. May the foot prints that we leave, lead them to believe and the lives we live inspire them to obey."

There is an old parental statement that has been used since time immemorial, "Don't do as I do, do as I say." That may give temporary relief from an awkward situation where our children may become aware of our hypocrisies and inconsistencies, but in the long run, our children will do what we do and not what we say. In fact, whatever we allow in moderation, our children tend to take to excess. This leads to the importance of adopting the correct education model to disciple our children.

The Meaning of Education

Education, in the Latin, means to pour in and to draw out. With our public schools' secular agenda, what is being poured into our children? What is being drawn out? Before you answer, keep in mind Jesus taught that we would discern the nature of things by the fruit it produces (Matthew 7:20). One just has to look at the condition of our public schools to realize there is a major problem. Our schools have become veritable war zones filled with violent behavior, sexual immorality, pagan philosophy, gross vulgarity, and blatant disrespect for parental authority.

There is a principle that nature abhors a vacuum. Whenever the knowledge of God is removed from the public life of a nation, violence and perversion always replaces Him. This is the inescapable lesson that preceded Noah's deluge (Genesis 6). America officially banished God from our government and from our schools in the 1960s. Into the void rushed every kind of unclean bird and doctrine of devils (1 Timothy 4:1; Revelation 18:2). Yet, Christians still insist on sending their lambs to be educated by wolves. Tragically, many of their young suffer physical, mental, and worst of all, spiritual harm.

In light of this deplorable situation, what should be the goal of education as far as it relates to raising godly kids in a godless age? John Milton, author of Paradise Lost, maintains, "The end of learning is to repair the ruin of our first parents by regaining to know God aright; and out of that knowledge to love Him, to imitate Him, and to be like Him." If any education system does not begin with this premise, my solemn advice is to flee and create one that does.

With Milton's insight as our backdrop, let us explore the historical basis of American Christian education. A good place to start is with Noah Webster, the father of American education. He was born in Hartford, Connecticut in 1758. According to Bill Federer, historian and author, Noah Webster was "Known as 'the schoolmaster of the Nation. Noah Webster published the first edition of his American Dictionary of the English Language in November of 1828. It contained the greatest number of Biblical definitions in any secular volume."

Webster wrote his dictionary based upon a Biblical worldview. Besides the Bible, and Bill Federer's America's God and Country: Encyclopedia of Quotations, the 1828 first edition of American Dictionary of the English Language should adorn your library. It is a tremendous resource.

Noah Webster defined education in this manner:

45

"The bringing up, as of a child, instruction; formation of manners. Education comprehends all that series of instruction and discipline, which is intended to enlighten the understanding, correct the temper, and form the manners and habits of youth, and fit them for usefulness in their future stations. To give children a good education in manners, arts and science, is important; to give them a religious education is indispensable; and an immense responsibility rests on parents and guardians who neglect these duties."

Notice Webster's first emphasis, when it comes to the important subject of education, is the training of children's character. Men are enamored with gifting, talent, and skill. God, however, is impressed with character. Education must build into our children the foundation of a godly character in order to prepare them for their future stations in this life. The scriptures teach the fear of the Lord is the beginning of knowledge and wisdom (Proverbs 1:7). The fear of the Lord inspires us to depart from evil (Proverbs 16:6). This establishes integrity, where a person's word is their bond.

Without the fear of the Lord impressed upon children's souls, there is no sound basis for education. Remove God and his Word from the education of our young and not only will there be no basis for true knowledge, wisdom, and understanding, but the time-honored principles that fashion godly character will be missing as well. In fact, remove the knowledge of God as the foundation of education and it is not education at all, but humanistic indoctrination and pagan socialization.

Secondly, Webster mentions that academics have a place in education, but it is secondary to religious training. Not only is Christian training the source for establishing godly character, it forms in children the discipline of a Biblical worldview. Every academic subject needs to be filtered through the grid of God's revelation. Children must discover the leading idea of every topic and trace it back to God and his Word.

To accomplish this noble goal in education, I highly recommend the Principle Approach methodology for teaching. It is bibliocentric, placing the Bible at the heart of each subject. You can learn more from the Foundation for American Christian Education. Their website is www.face.net. There you will discover the four Rs—research, reason, relate, and record. It was this model that defined much of the education of our Founding Fathers.

This educational process is not multiple choice, fill in the blank, or marking true or false. Education should not be a guessing game. It should produce Christian character and critical thinking skills based on Biblical truths. This important discipline is missing from most educational systems today. Public education today teaches what children should think, not how to think critically.

Lastly, Webster stated, "An immense responsibility rests on parents and guardians who neglect these duties." What is missing from this statement? Notice Webster does not mention the church or the state as the responsible parties for the education of the young. Webster, as opposed to his modern Christian counterparts, was Biblical in his orientation. He knew learning was not just an education issue, but an issue of jurisdiction.

Nowhere in the Bible does God ordain the state to teach children. Although the church can help supplement our children's education, the primary responsible party, according to God's Word, is the parents. The Bible clearly teaches that the primary government responsible for training children is family government. He does not recognize nor endorse any other jurisdiction. Unfortunately, this revelation, for the most part, does not even appear as a glitch on the American church's screen. This Biblical ignorance accounts for most of the causalities suffered by our Christian young today.

It is likely Webster was familiar with the great Shema found in Deuteronomy 6:4–9:

> "Hear, O Israel: the Lord our God is one Lord: And thou shalt love the Lord thy God with all thine heart, and with all thy soul, and with all thy might. And these words, which I command thee this day, shall be in thine heart: And thou shalt teach them diligently unto thy children, and shalt talk of them when thou sittest in thine house, and when thou walkest by the way, and when thou liest down, and when thou risest up. And thou shalt bind them for a sign upon thine hand, and they shall be as frontlets between thine eyes. And thou shalt write them upon the posts of thy house, and on thy gates."

Deuteronomy 32:46–47 reads:

> "And he said unto them, set your hearts unto all the words which I testify among you this day, which ye shall command your children to observe to do, all the words of this law. For it is not a vain thing for you; because it is your life: and through this thing ye shall prolong your days in the land, whither ye go over Jordan to possess it."

According to these passages from Deuteronomy, the greatest commandment is to love God and the greatest application of that commandment is home education. Moses declared this was not a vain thing; it was to be our life. How many Christians in America agree with Moses' assessment on the meaning of life? How many truly believe the meaning of the Christian life is to get married, stay faithful, have as many children God allows, and then home educate them for the glory of God and the advancement of his kingdom? (Psalm 127; Malachi 2:15).

Most Christians in America do not comprehend there is a major difference between the Biblical model of education, which is relational, versus the Greek model of education, which we see in America's school systems today. The Biblical model of education is discipleship and mentoring, while the Greek model is expediency, which merely views children as wards of the state. The Biblical model emphasizes God at its center. The Greek model emphasizes humanism. The Biblical model bonds the family. The Greek model bonds children to peers, teachers, and principles. The Biblical model nurtures honor for father and mother. The Greek model nurtures rebellion against father and mother. The Biblical model emphasizes principle, what is right, while the Greek model emphasizes pragmatism, what works, regardless if it is right or wrong. In the Greek model, the ends can justify the means.

According to Rosalie June Slater, author of the book The Family and the Nation—Biblical Childhood:

> "In no nation in the history of the Old Testament were children so conscientiously educated as were the children of (ancient) Israel. It was an education centered in religion and therefore all aspects and all subjects were related to knowledge of the Lord and His works, and to man's relationship to man in the light of God's principles."

Jesus, the great teacher, demonstrated this teaching style with his Apostles. He ate with them, walked with them, and lived with them. This was a part of his discipleship program. It was not a sterilized setting with classrooms segregated by age groups based upon an evolutionary model of education. No! Jesus taught God's message and modeled it before his disciples as a way of life. They in turn passed the truth of God to others as a way of life. This Kingdom educational program

49

was so effectual that the world labeled the early Christians as those "Who turned the world upside down" (Acts 17:6). Colossians 2:2–3 states:

"That their hearts might be comforted, being knit together in love, and unto all riches of the full assurance of understanding, to the acknowledgement of the mystery of God, and of the Father, and of Christ; In whom are hid all the treasures of wisdom and knowledge."

In Christ are hid all the treasures of wisdom and knowledge. Christian home education has this as its rock solid foundation. Every academic study should relate back to the Word of God and the wisdom it imparts. Homeschooling is designed to not only inculcate a multi-generational Kingdom vision into the hearts of our young, but to act as a protective barrier against the pagan philosophies designed to take captive unsuspecting minds.

In the same epistle, Paul warns, "See to it that no one takes you captive by philosophy and empty deceit, according to human tradition, according to the elemental spirits of the world, and not according to Christ" (Colossians 2:8). Paul furthers defines the pagan mind that controls much of public education. He states, "Now this I say and testify in the Lord, that you no longer walk as the Gentiles do, in the futility of their minds. They are darkened in their understanding, alienated from the life of God because of the ignorance that is in them, due to their hardness of heart" (Ephesians 4:17, 18).

Christian parents should embrace the godly task of rearing up critical thinkers like the men of Issachar, "who had understanding of the times, to know what Israel ought to do" (1 Chronicles 12:32). We must impart a vision and mission that will inspire the next generation of leaders to rise up and fulfill Isaiah 58:12:

"And they that shall be of thee shall build the old waste places: thou shalt raise up the foundations of many generations; and thou shalt be called, The repairer of the breach, The restorer of paths to dwell in."

Lastly, God's Word demands:

"Be ye not unequally yoked together with unbelievers: for what fellowship hath righteousness with unrighteousness? and what communion hath light with darkness? And what concord hath Christ with Belial? or what part hath he that believeth with an infidel? And what agreement hath the temple of God with idols? for ye are the temple of the living God; as God hath said, I will dwell in them, and walk in them; and I will be their God, and they shall be my people. Wherefore come out from among them, and be ye separate, saith the Lord, and touch not the unclean thing; and I will receive you, And will be a Father unto you, and ye shall be my sons and daughters,

If our nation is ever to have a new birth of freedom that secures a future and a hope for our posterity, we must obey God when it comes to the education of our children. Christians can no longer afford to prop up government's humanistic temple, which denies the existence of our Lord and teaches vain philosophies contrary to his truth. Christian children can no longer be used as grist that fuels the pagan mill of public education.

As God's Word declares, it is time to come out from among them and be separate. And as we do, keep in mind that home education is not a separation unto isolation, but a separation unto impact. If you desire to raise godly children in a godless age, you must separate your children from a godless system. If you obey and do things God's way, you will get

51

God's results. If you are tempted to do it the world's way, do not be shocked when you reap the world's results.

May Christians inspire a great exodus that will vacate American government schools. May God lead us out of the wilderness of public education into the Promise Land of home education. May it begin in earnest in our day. It is time to come out from the kingdom of darkness and live, think, and act like believing Christians. It is time to educate our children for the glory of God and the advancement of his kingdom in the earth.

Chapter Five:
Divine Order in the Home

"But I want you to understand that the head of every man is Christ, the head of a wife is her husband, and the head of Christ is God" (1 Corinthians 11:3).

Much of our marriages, families, culture, and our government are out of order, and thus we are spinning out of control. God is not the author of confusion. He is the God of design and order. He is also the God of extreme creativity who graciously added an aesthetic quality to His entire creation. He made things practical for our survival and yet made things beautiful for our enjoyment. He is indeed a great and good God. A wife that understands these creative aspects of God can duplicate them through a spirit of loveliness in her home.

The truth revealed in this chapter came to us in a profound way. Once we repented of our anti-child selfishness and began to trust God with our reproductive life, lo and behold, my wife became pregnant. We were, however, in a quandary as to where to have our first baby, Shekinah. Back then, our ability to provide was contingent on traveling in full time ministry. It was and remains to this day a life of faith to serve the Lord.

The hospital demanded that we stay local so they could monitor the pregnancy months before the delivery. Financially, that was not feasible. We prayed, researched, and sought counsel. A precious couple from our church gave us some resources on home births and prayed with us about the possibility of taking that course of action.

From what we could glean, there were people who chose home births, but only after having bad experiences in the hospital. This pregnancy, however, was our first. We had no previous experience to compare. It was all mysterious, excit-

53

ing, and a little disconcerting.

We did not slouch in preparation. We studied biology books, science books, and pregnancy books. We diligently looked up all covenant Scriptures concerning child birth. We wrote them out, meditated upon them, and prayed fervently. It was a big step of faith. In the midst of this situation, we providentially met an incredible lady who was a midwife. She was a grandma who helped usher in 150 babies kicking and screaming into this world. This was not her profession, but her ministry.

It is within that context she dropped a truth bomb that rocked our world. In order for her to take us on as a midwife, she had one crucial question. She asked, "Is your marriage in divine order?" She looked me squarely in the eye and asked, "Sir, can you honestly say that you love your wife as Christ loves His church? I'm not talking about a romantic love that produced this child, but a true, genuine, sacrificial love of God for your wife!"

As I fumbled to respond, she turned her eyes upon my wife and asked her, "Do you submit yourself to your husband as the church submits to Christ? Do you accept his headship as the lawful authority over your family?" After we caught our breath, we humbly told her that we were doing our best to live out the commands of our Lord in that regard.

After this challenge, I was curious why she asked these penetrating questions. She told us that she would never assist as a midwife unless the marriage she was serving was in divine order. Through years of experience she learned a rule of thumb. The more the marriage was in divine order, the less complications occurred at delivery. The less the marriage was in order, the more complications she experienced delivering babies. There are always exceptions to the rule, but she knew full well the pain and toil that women would experience when it came to child birth. She wanted to make sure that the woman was properly covered and submitted to her husband.

Genesis 3:16, 17 was the basis for her concerns. God's Word states, "To the woman He said, I will surely multiply your pain in child bearing; in pain you shall bring forth children. Your desire shall be for your husband and he shall rule over you."

The Battle of Sexes

There are two enemies that have conspired to neuter men and empower women to rebel to overthrow the divine order in the home. These two adversaries, male passivity and female dominance, has contributed greatly to the sexual confusion that is savaging our nation. We must understand this battle between the sexes rage from within and from without. We must squarely face and overcome these threats to prayerfully bring our families back to divine order.

The battle from within is the inherent weaknesses of men that has passed to all males since the Fall -passivity and irresponsibility. When the going gets tough, men take off. Men tend to be aggressive when it comes to their sinful, lustful, and selfish nature, but passive when it comes to advancing righteousness, godliness, and justice in the earth.

God's Word teaches, "Be angry, and do not sin: do not let the sun go down on your wrath" (Ephesians 4:26). "Be angry" is a command. It is tempered, however, by "do not sin." The problem with men is they are angry for all the wrong reasons and their wrath does not establish the righteousness of God (James 1:20). Men can get angry when things do not go their way. They can get upset when they feel people, including their wife, children, or situations "interrupt" their pursuits.

There is a godly reality called righteous indignation. In both Testaments, our Lord at times manifested this aspect of

55

His divine nature. One just has to recall Matthew 23 where our Lord excoriated the religious leaders of His time to realize Almighty God is capable of wrath, anger, and certain fiery judgements. Indeed, our God is a consuming fire and it is a fearful thing to fall into His hands (Hebrews 12:29, 10:31).

As Christians, it is vital to love what God loves and hate what he hates. God's Word reminds us, "Let those who love the Lord, hate evil" (Psalms 97:10). These virtues are keys to God's precious anointing (Hebrews 1:9). The prophet Isaiah taught that it was the anointing that destroys the yoke (Isaiah 10:27). It is therefore incumbent upon men as husbands and fathers to have God's Word instruct and the Holy Spirit guide our anger to produce Kingdom rather than destructive fruits in our lives.

In the book of Genesis, we learn when Adam's manhood was demanded of him, he went south. He stepped out of his realm of responsibility and obeyed his wife rather than God. The price of that treachery has been immense. He lost his God ordained authority to rule justly in the earth.

Mankind has paid a steep price for this rebellion. Sin, death, and hell invaded the earth and we have endured much suffering ever since. Apart from Christ's redemption, men and nations are condemned to experience the severe consequences that came from the Fall without any other remedy available.

The truth is God's authority always rests upon and works through men who take their place of responsibility. So many men are morally compromised in America today. They lack the moral courage to take a stand. There is a deficiency of moral authority to address and defeat the blood lust defiling our nation today. To overcome this deplorable condition, men must repent. Men must take serious their responsibility to do their duty as husbands and fathers. They must be actively engaged in the home, church, community, and culture.

This is the first major building block to restore divine order back in the home.

The battle from without is feminism. This leads to the inherent sinful tendency within women, which is to dominate, manipulate, and control the man. This hearkens back to the curse placed upon women discovered in Genesis 3:16, 17. Most "Christian" feminists falsely teach that the source of the curse on women is the husband ruling over them. This is far from the truth. That is actually the source of God's protection, provision, and care for women and children in our poor fallen world.

The source of the curse is the word "desire." This is the same word that God used to warn Cain before he murdered his brother Abel. Genesis 4:7 records, "If you do well, will you not be accepted? And if you do not do well, sin lies at the door. And its desire is for you, but you should rule over it." In other words, if you do not master your passions by obeying God, sin, like a lioness, will pounce, dominate, manipulate, and overtake you.

Furthermore, Isaiah 3:12 warns what happens when a nation's sayings and doings are against the Lord, "As for My people, children are their oppressors, and women rule over them. O My people! Those who lead you cause you to err, and destroy the way of your paths." Obviously, this wretched condition is not conducive in establishing a stable home that is in order.

We think we are a progressive and an enlightened nation as we send our women into battle, but little do we know, we are descending more and more into God's curse. Our nation is consciously rejecting patriarchy for the lie of feminism. If we continue in this rebellion, it is a harbinger of greater woe yet to come.

The battle of the sexes comes down to two issues. They are function and value. In salvation, according to Galatians

3:28, there is neither Jew nor Greek, (racial warfare) neither free nor slave, (social status) and neither male nor female (the battle between the sexes). We are all one in Christ. Men are not superior and women are not inferior in value. God loves us all the same in Christ.

It is in the arena of function that God puts major difference between men and women. According to 1 Corinthians 11:3, God's divine order is God, Christ, man, and woman. God presupposes strength and leadership to men. 1 Corinthians 16:13 states, "Watch ye, stand fast in the faith, quit ye like men, be strong." This is God challenging men to be men. He expects males to act a man's part in His Kingdom. God presupposes alertness, firmness, strength, courage, bravery, and gallantry in men who are rooted and grounded in the faith and love of God.

On the other hand, (And this maybe fighting words in today's feminized culture) God calls women, the weaker vessel (1 Peter 3:7). This truth is crucial to discern how men should treat women. Women are wired differently than men and thank God for this blessing. Women tend to be more talkative and emotionally oriented, while men tend to talk less and are less emotional. Again, there are always exceptions to the rule. This distinction, however, is one of the reasons why God demands that men do not become bitter against their wives (Colossians 3:19).

It is this revelation that has produced in the history of the church the notion of chivalry. It is just like the song goes, "I guess it is just the woman in you that brings out the man in me." A woman with a meek and mild spirit serves to tame and domesticate the wild beast in men (1 Peter 3:1-4). It helps turn them from predators to protectors.

A majority of women in America have abandoned their role and function as wives and mothers. The void left at home has proven disastrous. Tragically, most women today are

58

being conditioned to be aggressive to compete in a "man's world." As a result, we are raising men who biologically can have children as Voddie Baucham has astutely observed. The results are more and more American men are looking to other nations for brides. They are done with the liberated American woman.

Historically, women were gifted by God to absorb some of the harshness of life and somehow grant a measure of comfort, nurturing, and gentleness in our poor-fallen world. Since women have left home for more fulfilling chores, life has become intolerable for the modern family. Who remains to bind the wounds of life, if mothers abandon their children to godless systems that raise them in her stead? Because the church has not looked squarely at these issues and dealt with them Biblically, it has served to undermine the building block of our society, the family.

It has also created a national security crisis. John Adams, our second president observed:

> From all that I had read of history and government of human life and manners, I had drawn this conclusion, that the manners of women were the most infallible barometer to ascertain the degree of morality and virtue of a nation. The Jews, the Greeks, the Romans, the Swiss, the Dutch, all lost their public spirit and their republican forms of government when they lost the modesty and domestic virtues of their women.

Dealing with Disagreements within the Family

Hopefully, by now you see the importance of the authority structure and are convinced of God's order in the home. In the Old Testament, God ordered a one year honeymoon for couples to get to know each other (Deuteronomy 24:5).

In our day, if we take a week long honeymoon, we are fortunate. God knew it would take at least a year for two selfish people thrust in the crucible of a marriage covenant to work things out. He knew it would require some holy friction to establish how to relate to each other in a God ordained home. Surely, it takes some time for wisdom to build its house and set up its pillars (Proverbs 9:1, 24:3).

There are three main areas which provide the three-legged stool upon which a healthy marriage is built and tested. They are communication, finances, and sex. Not necessarily in that order. One leg fails and typically the entire stool collapses. There may be other challenges, but these seem to be the top three major causes for problems that can ill affect a marriage if not handled properly.

To handle disagreements in these areas as well as others, God's divine order in the home provides helpful guidance to settle disputes. In dealing with worldly situations, conventional wisdom is to follow the money trail. In the home, follow the responsibility trail. The one that God holds responsible is the one who must have the authority to make final decisions. In family government, the one responsible before God is the husband and father. Therefore, he must exercise godly authority as a servant leader.

Now, it is important that every good leader have a confidant that will prayerfully provide good counsel and sound wisdom. There may be other good men, pastors, and elders that can provide sound counsel and good advice, but ultimately in the home, it should be the wife. She should act as an extra set of eyes and ears to be a faithful helpmate to her husband in the midst of life's challenges.

Proverbs is clear on this principle. God's Word teaches, "Plans are established by counsel; by wise counsel wage war" (Proverbs 20:18). It is a foolish leader who rejects this principle. His pride, arrogance, and foolishness will be his undo-

60

ing. Rejecting or neglecting godly counsel will not just impact him, but all who depend on him. The Bible and history are replete with examples of entire families destroyed based upon the sin, disobedience, and folly of men.

When faced with dilemmas, a married couple should begin in prayer and then discuss the situation. It is good for the husband to ask his wife her take on the situation. However, there is a divine tension in doing so that one must keep in mind. There were a few times when God rebuked men for hearkening to the voice of their wives, rather than obeying His voice (Genesis 3:7, 16:2). There were times as well when God commended the man for listening to his wife's advice (Genesis 21:12).

How do we discern the difference? All counsel must be ultimately weighed and judged by God's word. It is important for men to lead courageously with God's word like the second Adam, Jesus our Lord (Matthew 4:1-11). Otherwise, we are stuck in the condition of the first Adam, which is passivity and irresponsibility. Men must think principally, governmentally, and jurisdictionally to receive guidance to make wise decisions in the midst of murkiness, deception, and error.

As it pertains to the wife, it is important for her to give good, godly counsel as a helpmate. It would be unwise for the husband to not listen or validate her opinions. But that is where it must end. After that, her role is primarily one of intercession. She needs to undergird her husband and family in prayer.

The problem is many women want to go further than giving counsel and prayer. They desire to replace the Holy Spirit in a man's life. They are not just content to give their opinion, but demand their way. Their chosen weapons to secure their will are to deny sex or nag until the man yields (Samson anyone?). If she wins, she gets what she wants, but finds she cannot live with the results (Proverbs 21:9, 25:24). Tragically, she will end up despising her soft, indecisive husband in her heart and undress him publicly amongst her friends. I've seen this scenario lived out more than I care to remember. Many men have forfeited God's call upon their lives in order to appease their wives. It never ends well.

Sometimes women just need to let men fail. Men need to grow up and learn responsibility. If a woman keeps demanding her way, the man will do one of two things. He will either retreat to the default setting of passivity and irresponsibility or if he still has some testosterone left, he will fight back. Either way, it is a lose/lose situation for the health and soundness of the family.

Marriage is supposed to be a place of harmony, not competition. In the family, at least in times past, men tended to be concerned about justice and what is right or wrong. They used to be the disciplinarian in the home. Whereas, women tended to be more the nurturers that were mercy orientated. Together, parents exercising different attributes of God's character, justice and mercy, raised godly children. In many cases today that model has been disregarded or the genders have reversed roles. Much of the sexual confusion and immorality can be traced to this rebellion against God's order in the home.

Keep a United Front

As children multiply in the home, the battlefront will change, which will also impact the divine order of the home. If you have settled the roles Biblically between husband and wife, it is now time to settle the roles Biblically between parents and children. Like us, our children are born with a selfish, sinful nature. They become masters at an early age to sense and exploit any perceived differences between Mom and Dad. They have no problem exploiting those differences

62

to get their own way.

We see this most painfully in cases of divorce. The parents tend to use their children to harm their ex-spouse, while children use the compromise of their divorced parents to be indulged. Divorced parents must prove their love by giving the children what they demand. It is a hellish scenario that has become the norm for many in our broken, wounded land.

As parents, it is crucial that you keep a united front and stay on the same page in dealing with your children. If you have any disagreements concerning them, it is important that you do not discuss or argue those differences in front of your children. They will use that to their advantage. Most will work one against the other to get their own selfish way. Go behind closed doors and preferably hammer it out quietly and discreetly. Pray, discuss and reach a just and righteous decision. Together, implement a godly plan of action.

Children need boundaries. They are prone to challenge boundaries. When you reinforce godly parameters, children may initially kick against the goads, but in the long run it provides a measure of safety and security (Acts 26:14). This is a great benefit to the order of the home.

It is important when training your children in this manner that you are selective on which hill you are prepared to die on. Some parents micro mange children and their behavior to the point children can't breathe. We chose to not approach child training in that manner. I've seen parents lose children for being too loose and for being too strict. One has to be wise to determine when to let go of the reins a bit and when to jerk them back into reality.

Our method to choose what hill to die on was contingent on perceived patterns of disobedience and not just sporadic failures in their conduct. Though we did correct failure, it was the pattern of disobedience that required the hill to die

63

on. Going to bed at night, fussiness with food, patterns of laziness, constant wandering of the mind, bickering, disrespect, and other areas demanded attention. Discipline, keeping a united front, and a plan of action were then warranted. There will be more on discipline, but these tidbits are in keeping with divine order in the home.

Another pointer that may help, Dad and Mom, seek to be affectionate with each other in front of your children. My children used to flock to us when we as parents showed some modest form of intimacy. They wanted to get in on the holy huddle. As my wife and I hugged or smooched, the children would run to grab our legs and try to get into the middle of our lovefest. This provided tremendous security for their souls and also helped to stabilize order in our home.

Manly Admonishments

These last recommendations are written to the man of the house. To have peace fill your home, you must remember that it is not always about being right, but loving. You should seek to have a tender relationship with your family, though you must discipline your children when needed and necessary.

Case in point, there were times when my wife and I had disagreements. I was 100 % right and she was 100 % wrong. I had the backing of the throne of God, His revealed truth and all the angels in my corner. This, in and of itself, did not heal the rift nor repair the breach ill affecting our relationship.

It was at the point, providentially, I came across a Scripture that gave me the much needed guidance to restore peace, harmony and order in our home. God's Word stated, "We love Him, because He first loved us" (1 John 4:19). As I mediated on this revelation, it dawned on me, who is more right than God? Who is more wrong than His fallen creatures? Yet, in the midst of this alienation, it was God who initiated the

64

peace process to restore our broken relationship.

A true shepherd is not a hireling but lays down his life for the sheep. Husbands ought to humbly lead and follow this example. We need to be man enough to initiate the peace process to restore the shalom (peace and order) of our homes. It is crucial to secure your wife, drive out the enemy, repair the breach, and restore the home in Jesus' name! Do not let the sun go down on your wrath (Ephesians 4:26)

Can a woman take advantage of this to dominate her husband? Yes, she can. At least, you will know what spirit you are dealing with in attempting to bring a righteous resolve to the conflict. Other issues may surface as well. Appropriate measures can then be implemented to deal with them properly. Ignoring them, however, will never make them go away. It is only by obeying God and honoring His word that couples can resolve issues in a godly manner.

Next, we have raised our 13 children on the front lines of the battle for the souls of men, the lives of babies, and the future of our blood stained, perverted nation. Some people choose small families and big ministry or small ministry and large families. By God's grace, we chose both.

Most of our life consists of juggling many responsibilities. We have to keep up with many spinning plates in life. We were and continue to be a very busy homeschool family and frontline ministry. No regrets. Our family with all its warts has, is, and always will be our greatest source of wellbeing that sweeps over us like a wave.

As a man, husband, father, and minister, the Lord blessed me to be able to handle dangerous, intense, and threatening situations with a lot of poise. However, the Scriptures teach, it is the little foxes that spoil the vineyard (Song of Solomon 2:15). Sometimes the pressure was so intense in the battle that I was reduced to a zombie state. No sleep, no food, no bodily functions, just a blank stare. During those times of the dark night of the soul, it was difficult to even formulate words to put into a prayer. Nothing for a time could relieve the excruciating pain endured in the battle that raged from within and without.

Family life did not take a vacation while experiencing redemptive suffering for the cause of Christ (Matthew 6:33). In the midst of this, as children are prone to do, they would pull some boneheaded folly. To my shame and disgrace, I would unload all my frustration, pressure, and stress upon them. Now, they were wrong for what they did. But as the old saying goes, "Two wrongs never make a right." I was wrong on how I responded to their disobedience.

The Scriptures teach, "Confess your trespasses to one another, and pray for one another, that you may be healed. The effective, fervent prayer of a righteous man avails much (James 5:16). There were times when I had to get down on my knees in front on my children and humbly repent. I told them I was wrong for behaving that way and asked for their forgiveness. Gratefully, they were always more than willing to release my foolish outbursts.

To be honest, it was moments like those that did more to secure their love, respect, and honor for me and God than perhaps all my teaching of God's word combined. They knew Dad was not perfect, but he was a genuine Christian who loved God and obeyed His word, even when wrong. It was the modeling of Christianity, combined with godly teaching and storming the gates of hell that secured our children in the faith.

This last recommendation took me years to understand. It came like all other nuggets from heaven in a profound way. This life lesson came when my second daughter, Cassia, was getting married to my son-in-love, Robby. He is a faithful son whom I love and appreciate dearly. So far, they have blessed us with five grandchildren.

It was at their rehearsal dinner. The press was pestering me in doing an interview. We were in the fires of the battle as usual. I had to look up to see the bottom of the barrel. We could not afford the wedding and on and on it went. It was truly a tough time.

Then, as I'm walking into the church, I saw my daughter stunningly beautiful shining like an angel before me. All the pressure, stress, and anxiety filling my head were still in red alert mode, but there she was, a vision of loveliness. What's a man to do?

It was at that point that I consciously had to make a serious decision. I could remain defeated in my mind. I could let circumstances bounce me to and fro. I could continue to let situations dominate my life to the point it would rob me of God moments or I could cast my cares upon the Lord and enter in the joyous festivities.

I'm glad to report that I chose the latter. It was a glorious decision. The circumstances did not change, but my ability to deal with those situations dramatically changed. We must remember, there are things within our control and things outside our control. Be diligent to take care of issues within your control and trust God for those things outside of your control. Continue to bear good Kingdom fruit and know that God will vindicate and make a way in His time.

I've learned that it is not the challenges, pressures, stresses, attacks, persecutions, and tribulations that ultimately matters in life, but how we respond that makes all the difference in the world. It will determine defeat or victory. Choose wisely, man of the house.

Chapter Six: Discipline

"My son, do not despise the chastening of the Lord, nor be discouraged when you are rebuked by Him; for whom He the Lord loves He chastens, and scourges every son whom He receives" (Hebrews 12:5, 6).

To discipline properly, you must first establish a standard by which to judge transgression. First and foremost that standard is God's law/word. But how does that breakdown in mentoring your children at home? Ah, now there is the rub.

The standard we chose as parents is for our children to obey quickly and quietly the first time. It is indeed a high standard and one that took diligence to enforce. I'm not sure if we completely obtained it, but it was a worthwhile goal to achieve when it came to the discipline of our children.

Words like scourge and chasten in our opening verse do not go over very well in our Peter Pan, (never grow up syndrome) bubble wrapped generation of perpetual immaturity. It seems harsh, even cruel on the surface. The Greek word for chasten means flogged and scourge reinforces the idea. Jesus on the cross gives us a powerful word picture of what it looks like to endure intense, off the charts scourging. Not a pretty sight for sure.

This happened to the perfect, obedient Son of the living God and in our narcissistic love of self, do we think we shall escape the discipline of the Lord? I've been to God's wood shed too many times and have learned answer to that question. How about you my friend?

In giving this illustration, I'm not suggesting child abuse. I'm merely pointing out the fact that when God sets His love on someone, one of the signs is He "scourges every son whom He receives." The text goes on to reveal that without this loving discipline, we are bastards without a loving Father who claims us as His own (Hebrews 12:8).

My children have learned that because God loves them, they will not get away with evil. They may be able to con us, friends, the church and our society, but they can never con God. He beholds the good and the evil and will render to every man what is due (Proverbs 15:3; Romans 2:6). Based upon these and other passages, we exhorted our children to live for an audience of one, the Holy One.

To reveal all the times our children escaped us in their sin, but got busted by the Lord are too numerous to count. Suffice it to say, they ended up knowing full well that God loved them. They eventually came to rest in His love. This helped to develop the inner monitoring system that reinforced one of our golden rules at home. Self-government is the key to liberty. There will be more on that topic later.

The Rod

God has different symbols for His authority in the governments that he established for His glory and our benefit. There are four basic governments. They are self, family, church, and civil government. Some would include educational and vocational realms as governments as well. In self-government, baptism is an act of obedience. It publicly testifies that we have submitted to Christ's Lordship and now identify with Him as a committed follower. This touches on self-government.

In church government, God's authority is symbolized by keys. Keys lock and unlock. In this case, these keys unlock and permit people into God's Kingdom. If they persist in unrepentant, open, flagrant sin, those same keys can be used to excommunicate guilty parties (Matthew 18:15-20).

1 Corinthians and 2 Corinthians serve as a case study in church discipline. The Apostle Paul dealt with an offending member of the Corinthian church. This church refused to

discipline the offender. The Apostle Paul made it crystal clear on what was expected by God when there is a danger of a little leaven (open rebellious sin), leavening the entire lump (The local church of the living God). He called for the church to rise up and remove the person responsible for committing an act that would have caused the heathen to blush (1 Corinthians 5:1).

Specifically, he stated, "In the name of our Lord Jesus Christ, when you are gathered together, along with my spirit, with the power of our Lord Jesus Christ, deliver such a one to Satan for the destruction of the flesh, that his spirit may be saved in the day of the Lord Jesus" (1 Corinthians 5:4, 5).

It is rare in these days that the Church would exercise this kind of discipline to correct the church that others might fear (1 Timothy 5:20). It may cost too many parishioners and their tithes. However, what happens to God's care for His church and even His love for the offending member when the church fails to discipline?

In the Corinthian case, the discipline worked. The church, however, was once again slow to comprehend their duty. Paul had to now guide them to restore the man back to right standing with God and His Church (2 Corinthians 1:3-11). The person in question brought forth fruits meet for repentance by exercising godly sorrow. It was not worldly sorrow that was primarily concerned about being caught and suffering consequences.

It was a godly sorrow that produced these righteous results, "For observe this very thing, that you sorrowed in a godly manner: What diligence it produced in you, what clearing of yourselves, what indignation, what fear, what vehement desire, what zeal, what vindication! In all things you proved yourselves to be clear in this matter" (2 Corinthians 7:11). It is important that you train your children to know the difference between worldly sorrow and godly sorrow. Feeling sorry for oneself or true repentance hangs in the balance.

The symbol of God's authority in civil government is the sword. It is not a pencil, which the state uses to teach children. That is not within the purview of their delegated authority. Education comes under the jurisdiction of family government. Neither is it a spoon to bilk tax payers to set up their federal plantation called the welfare state.

The civil government is supposed to be a ministry of justice. It is ordained as a minister of God, the Deacon of the Lord. Its divine purpose is to punish evildoers and protect the good citizens of the land. Of course, it must be Almighty God and His holy commandments that define for mankind the concepts of good and evil. Otherwise, the depravity of man has the capacity to insist that good is evil and evil, good (Isaiah 5:20). Once evil is codified into law, tyranny raises its ugly head.

The sword represents lawful coercive force to establish a just social order. Its divine purpose is to ensure mankind never returns to the pre-condition wicked state before the flood (Genesis 6). Civil government's primary objective Biblically is to protect life and stop the shedding of innocent blood (Genesis 9:6). This provides a semblance of stability in a fallen world filled with sin that leads to criminality.

In the home, the symbol of God's authority is the rod. There are times when the board of education must be applied to the seat of learning. The book of Proverbs is replete with exhortations to faithfully wield the rod at home. Most Americans, including those who name the name of Christ view this as child abuse. God, however, thinks otherwise. He views the withholding of the rod when it is necessary as child abuse.

Here are some Scriptures to ponder:

"He who spares his rod hates his son, but he who loves him disciplines him promptly" (Proverbs 13:24).

71

"Foolishness is bound up in the heart of a child; the rod of correction will drive it far from him" (Proverbs 22:15).

"Do not withhold correction from a child, for if you beat him with a rod, he will not die. You shall beat him with a rod, and deliver his soul from hell" (Proverbs 23:13, 14).

Most parents today choose the big "time out" to "discipline" their wayward children or remove something they like. America's justice system is based upon this model. We put criminals in "time out" called jail and take away their freedom. Unless the Lord saves them while in confinement, jail, most of the time, just serves to make them more cunning criminals.

Biblically, God's system of justice consisted of capital punishment, corporeal punishment (A rod for the back of fools), and restitution (Proverbs 10:13). There were Cities of Refuge that was the closest to our model of a prison system. It was more like a holding center till the authorities could determine the possible guilt or innocence when a killing had taken place. They had to determine the nature of the killing. Was it murder, self-defense, or accidental death? Their findings determined the appropriate course of action. If the suspect was found innocent, the person was released, if found guilty, the person was put to death.

There were several other capital crimes that could lead to capital punishment in the Old Testament. There were strict measures in place, however, to protect the rights of the accused before capital punishment could be enforced. Murder was the only crime worthy of death that the criminal could not escape the death penalty. There is no ransom for the murderer (Numbers 35:31).

Putting children in time out typically produces a seething time with no merciful closure or righteous resolve that releases them from their infractions. Most children do not learn the lessons of discipline in this manner. While alone in their room most flail around desperately seeking relief from the guilt they refuse to acknowledge. In time out, most learn self-pity, a woe is me attitude, and a steady growth of despising their parents in their hearts, which can cleverly be disguised.

Disobedience brings Pain

We know from Scripture that the wages of sin is death (Romans 6:23). Sin can lead to sickness, disease, and early death. Sin can consume us with shame, guilt, regret, remorse, unforgiveness, and a variety of other miseries that takes its toll on our minds and bodies. For instance, Proverbs 14:30 teaches, "A sound heart is life to the body, but envy is rottenness to the bones." This is part of the reason why healing was included in the Lord's atonement (Isaiah 53).

James 5:14, 15 connect the dots, "Is anyone among you sick? Let him call for the elders of the church, and let them pray over him, anointing him with oil in the name of the Lord. And the prayer of faith will save the sick, and the Lord will raise him up. And if he has committed sins, he will be forgiven."

Our Lord verified sickness can be associated with sin. It can also spring from Satan (Luke 13:16). Sickness can manifest merely for the glory of God (John 9:3). This last one is a little more controversial in some segments of the church. Sickness can come as God's judgment upon people who refuse to repent of gross immorality (Revelation 2:20-23).

In healing the man that was paralytic, Jesus declared, "Which is easier, to say, 'Your sins are forgiven you,' or to say, 'Rise up and walk'? But that you may know that the Son of Man has power on earth to forgive sins"—He said to the man who was paralyzed, "I say to you, arise, take up your bed, and

73

go to your house" (Luke 5:23, 24). After healing another man, He warned, "See, you have been made well. Sin no more, lest a worse thing come upon you" (John 5:1-15, 8:11).

The bottom line purpose for the rod is to establish this reality to our children, disobedience brings pain. God has provided on the anatomy of our children the exact spot to reach their souls with this unavoidable truth. He gave us all a cushion called the behind. You should not strike any other part of the body. It is there, the rod is to be faithfully applied. Not a hand, lest you confuse the child. The hands are for caressing, comfort, and healing. All this, of course, should be age appropriate.

Spanking reinforces the reality that disobedience brings pain. God wants children in the merciful, loving setting of a Christian home to learn this valuable lesson early in life. If they refuse discipline at home, life will reinforce its unmistakable reality. The problem with life, however, it doesn't give a rip about our welfare. It will crush us without mercy as we delude ourselves and ignore this important life lesson.

The Scriptures teach that there is pleasure in sin for a season. Once the season is done, however, it is payback time (Hebrews 11:25). If our children do not hearken at home and continue to reject this life lesson out of the home, eternity will settle it forever. Hell is God's final answer to all those who reject the premise that disobedience brings pain. Perhaps, this is why the passage in Proverbs specifically states, "You shall beat him with a rod, and deliver his soul from hell" (Proverbs 23:14).

Other Disciplinary Tools

You may be questioning if spanking is the silver bullet or the magic wand that solves all disciplinary problems. The short answer is no. There are other means that are also important to faithfully mentor your child. We have touched on

74

some of them previously.

On the chapter concerning education, one of the objectives was to correct the "temper of the youth" to prepare them for their future stations in life. This means we have to go the extra mile to forge godly character in the life of our children.

There are other tools in the tool box. One of them is Pete and repeat. This requires incredible patience on the part of parents. Most of the time, our teaching, instruction, and training will go in one ear and right out the other without registering in the souls of our children. Just like God set up continual reminders, memorials, and Ebenezer Stones throughout His Word based upon the forgetfulness of men, so we must also put our children in remembrance (1 Samuel 7:12). How long? Till the penny drops and they get it.

I could remember my first wife struggling to homeschool our children based upon this dilemma. Our children's need for loving discipline was constant. Their disobedience was always "interrupting" their education and training. We decided that this was not an interruption or set back but was indeed, a major part of our attempts to educate our children. At the end of the day, the reality comes down to this. We, as parents, receive the worst our children have to offer, so God and this world can receive their best.

Faithful teaching, persistent instruction, and dependable training coupled with the rod go a long way to raise children in the fear and admonishment of the Lord. Simultaneously, keep your eye on the prize, which is, children obey quickly and quietly the first time from the heart.

There is a story that can help drive home this point. There was a woman at a mall trying to keep up with her rambunctious son. She demanded the boy sit down. He continued to run rampant. Finally, she grabbed him and sat him down. The boy defiantly looked into his mother's eyes and shouted, "I may be sitting down on the outside, but I'm still standing up on the inside."

The lesson here acknowledges that we can get our children to perform outwardly for a season, but still not reach the heart. It is there, the inward part, that God desires His truth to reside (Psalms 51:6). We can manipulate our children's behavior based upon rewards and withholding benefits from them. I would exercise caution in using that approach.

Parents need to avoid treating children like Palov's dog experiment. If you recall, this method was also known as Classical Conditioning. Palov used dogs to highlight a learning procedure. He took a biologically potent incentive (in this case, food) and he connected it to a previously neutral stimulus, a bell. Eventually, when he rang the bell, the dogs would salivate, and he would feed them. This became the basis for the foundation of behaviorism, which led to a specific school of psychology in the mid-twentieth century.

Obviously, our children are not animals in a zoo, (Though sometimes it makes one wonder). Children are made in the image of God being raised in our homes. This means we should treat them differently from animals. They are not to be experimented on, but proactively trained to walk in the word, will, and way of the Lord.

The How of Loving Discipline

It is important that we do not discipline in anger. If your children's disobedience truly upsets you, it is time to walk away to gain your composure. Breathe, pray and then take on the task set before you.

The stars need not be in perfect alignment to incorporate the following process I suggest to discipline your children. In an imperfect world, other factors may rush in to disrupt your normal method to lovingly, but firmly right the wrongs in our children's behavior.

First, we really do not graduate to true parenting till we

76

have more than one child. With one, the guilty offender is self-evident. After one, parents need to become detectives to discern who is culpable and who is innocent in any dispute. Children are masters at half-truths to vindicate themselves and place the blame on others. Like a court room, we must have the truth, the whole truth, and nothing but the truth, so help us God! Children must learn that we cannot fix a lie, but only build on truth.

Once you determine the guilty party or parties, the dreaded moment arrives. It is time to call the child to the bedroom to face the music. Once there, take the time to point out their sin. Emphasize the nature of what they did that was wrong. Not based upon your arbitrary standard, but according to the infallible standard of God's Word.

This is really important. Hebrews 12:9, 10 teaches, "Furthermore, we have had human fathers who corrected us, and we paid them respect. Shall we not much more readily be in subjection to the Father of spirits and live? For they indeed for a few days chastened us as seemed best to them, but He for our profit, that we may be partakers of His holiness."

Notice, human fathers, most of the time, discipline their children based upon their whims or as what seemed best to them. It is critical your children know the difference between what upsets you and what violates the commandment of God. The ultimate goal is not what satisfies you as a parent, but what establishes the Holy fear of God in your children's lives. This is what will compel them to ultimately depart from evil that can destroy their lives (Proverbs 16:6).

Though what your children do may upset you, do not emphasize that aspect of it to discharge disciplinary measures. Point out Biblically their failure by demonstrating their breaking one or more of the commandments of God. It just might be they did not honor you as father or mother.

Once the infraction is established, it is time for the rod to

77

be applied. This may take training as well, but it is time for the child or children to "assume the position." This means the offending party must grab the bed and stand still while applying the rod. This is for their protection as well as the parents. When a child flails about, the danger of hurting the child or ourselves increases dramatically. To be safe, they must learn to assume the position.

After the spanking, which they must feel in order to be effective, it is time to reassure your love to them. Take them in your arms, hold them, caress them, point out what they did wrong, lead them to confession and then forgive them. Use these reconciliation times to reinforce their teaching, training, and instruction.

Always remind them of the 5th commandment, which is the first commandment with a promise from God, "Children, obey your parents in the Lord, for this is right. Honor your father and mother, which is the first commandment with promise: that it may be well with you and you may live long on the earth" (Ephesians 6:1-3). Impressing this truth on your children's souls will be helpful as you seek to raise godly children in a godless age.

Chapter Seven:
The Fifth Commandment

"Honor your father and your mother, that your days may be long upon the land which the LORD your God is giving you" (Exodus 20:12).

We left off the last chapter by acknowledging the role of the 5th commandment in child training. This chapter will go a little deeper. The word honor from this passage comes from a Hebrew word that means "to be heavy" or "to give weight." There are many influences, acquaintances, associates and friends that will come and go in your children's lives. They will find that only a few will be true friends that stick closer than a brother (Proverbs 18:24).

In general, people deserve a measure of honor since man is made in the image of God. God also commands us to give honor to whom honor is due, especially, if they are indeed honorable (Romans 13:7). Out of these human relationships deserving some semblance of honor, God places a high premium on the honor due parents. If children never obtain this virtue, they are less likely to honor God or anybody else for that matter.

Proverbs warns, "He who mistreats his father and chases away his mother is a son who causes shame and brings reproach… Whoever curses his father or his mother, his lamp will be put out in deep darkness… The eye that mocks his father, and scorns obedience to his mother, the ravens of the valley will pick it out, and the young eagles will eat it" (Proverbs 19:26, 20:20, 30:17). Obviously, Proverbs presents intense language and imagery associated with mistreating parents.

Moses specifically addressed the plague of rebellious children that dishonor parents when he established the case laws in Israel. It was a serious matter (Deuteronomy 21:18-21).

If a child would dare to raise his hand to strike a parent, the death penalty was recommended (Exodus 21:15). Why so harsh? Evidently, a child willing to rebel and strike a parent would prove detrimental to society.

Clearly, God was deeply concerned about this particular law in the Old Testament. He commanded honor for parents. He had strong denunciations and penalties in place for disrespecting them.

Out of the entire Decalogue in which the 5th commandment is found, God grants no special promise in loving and honoring Him. This truth is amazing. He waits till the 5th commandment on the human side of the tablets to grant a special promise. Children would live long and well on the earth, if they obeyed their parents in the Lord (Ephesians 6:1-3). Once again, the God of the Bible astounds us with His priorities and value system. By the way, these promises are good incentives to keep reminding your children as you train them in righteousness.

What about the New Testament? How important was this command to Jesus? The Gospel according to Mark grants some insight. Mark 7:9-13 records:

> He said to them, all too well you reject the commandment of God, that you may keep your tradition. For Moses said, 'Honor your father and your mother'; and, 'He who curses father or mother, let him be put to death.' But you say, 'If a man says to his father or mother, "Whatever profit you might have received from me is Corban"—' (that is, a gift to God), then you no longer let him do anything for his father or his mother, making the word of God of no effect through your tradition which you have handed down. And many such things you do.

In the New Testament, Jesus exposed the failure of the re-

80

ligious leaders who made the commandments of God of no effect by emphasizing their man-made traditions. Apparently, they had taken monies children were supposed to use to support their aging parents and made it Corban (a gift to God). Jesus rebuked them for violating family government to prosper church government. They gave money to God at the expense of taking care of their parents.

If one wonders whether Jesus is the Second Person of the Godhead, the true and living God, look no further than this account. It would prove far too tempting for Satan and false religions to reject such a gift. In fact, they would probably have demanded more. Not so with the God of the Bible. He is a God of all justice and will not be bribed (Deuteronomy 16:19). You do not steal from parents to bless God. He will not accept it. It violates the 5th commandment.

Jesus was committed to this commandment even till the end of His life here on earth. When He was hanging on the cruel cross becoming the propitiation for our sins, He went the extra mile to fulfill it (1 John 2:2, 4:10). In agony, He looked upon His mother and commanded the Apostle John to take care of her. With His remaining few breaths, He made sure He honored His mother in regard to the commandment that He instituted for His glory and our good (John 19:25-27). We should do no less.

There is something interesting about our Lord's commitment to His mother, however, when it comes to the 5th commandment. As you may know, there are children who feel justified in forsaking their aging parents due to mistreatment, abuse or a host of other issues growing up. Maybe, in extreme cases, that course may be proper due to physical or moral safety issues that could jeopardize other loved ones within the family. It is important to know, however, that our Lord was not a stranger to this dilemma.

His mother, Mary, according to the Angel Gabriel, was

81

blessed amongst women (Luke 1:28). Yet, she did not always handle the truth of her visitation according to knowledge. Though she pondered in her heart the glorious truths spoken to her directly about the Babe she was carrying in her womb, there were indeed struggles along the way (Luke 2:19).

There appears, at times, that she was overly concerned with the public fallout following her controversial Son. It was one thing to get the divine message from Gabriel and the prophetic confirmations from Simeon and Anna, but when her Son took on the powers that be, bearing the reproach of following Him became more difficult.

If you recall, the religious leaders threatened anyone who publicly followed our Lord and acknowledged that He was Messiah. They would excommunicate them from the synagogue and be summarily shunned in the community (John 9:22).

Mary's Son rebuked and challenged the religious and civil systems of His day on a continual basis. He set them back on their heels time and again. He called a Gentile woman seeking healing for her daughter a dog (Matthew 15:26). Could you imagine a preacher saying that today? He called the Pharisees, the religious leaders of His day, whited sepulchers and snakes (Matthew 23:33). He even called a political leader, Herod, a fox (Luke 13:32). He turned over the money changer's tables at the Temple of God and drove out them with a whip (John 2:15).

It was incidences like these that inspired the "powers that be" to question, "By what authority are you doing these things (Mark 11:28)? They knew that He spoke and acted as if He was Almighty God in the flesh (John 8:58, 59). When the reality of that conflict became apparent, it appears too difficult for Mary to handle. She faltered. Not only her, but Jesus' brethren as well.

Consider Matthew 12:46-50:

While He was still talking to the multitudes, behold, His mother and brothers stood outside, seeking to speak with Him. Then one said to Him, "Look, Your mother and Your brothers are standing outside, seeking to speak with You." But He answered and said to the one who told Him, "Who is My mother and who are My brothers?" And He stretched out His hand toward His disciples and said, "Here are My mother and My brothers! For whoever does the will of My Father in heaven is My brother and sister and mother."

Why is the Lord's family outside this meeting? Why are they not eager participants in His teachings? Clearly, there was an offence that caused separation. Notice, our Lord did not at this point even acknowledge they were a part of His earthly family. He merely stretched out His hands to the actual people seeking to obey His teaching and acknowledged them as those intimately related to Him.

It had to be even harder for our Lord's siblings. Could you imagine growing up in the same house as Jesus, the PER-FECT SON OF GOD? No sin, no flaw, and no moral defects to exploit. How could you tattletale on your big brother? The pressure of being compared to that perfect standard in your home would prove insurmountable.

According to the human condition, the envy, jealousy, and perhaps, even hatred, would be hard to mask. For a truth, those who walk according to the flesh tend to persecute those who walk according to the Spirit (Galatians 4:29). Keep in mind, this conflict will manifest in your home as some will indeed seek to honor and obey, while other children may be more obstinate.

In John 7:1-7, we read of this heated debate between Jesus and His brothers:

After these things Jesus walked in Galilee; for He did

83

After these things Jesus walked in Galilee; for He did not want to walk in Judea, because the Jews sought to kill Him. Now the Jews' Feast of Tabernacles was at hand. His brothers therefore said to Him, "Depart from here and go into Judea, that Your disciples also may see the works that You are doing. For no one does anything in secret while he himself seeks to be known openly. If You do these things, show Yourself to the world." **For even His brothers did not believe in Him.** Then Jesus said to them, "My time has not yet come, but your time is always ready. The world cannot hate you, but it hates Me because I testify of it that its works are evil.

Notice the brothers did not consider themselves disciples nor followers of the Lord at this point. They were literally baiting Him to go to a religious ceremony, knowing full well, it would place his life in danger. Talk about sibling rivalry? Yikes! In the case of Jesus' earthly family, it was taken to an extreme level.

What can we glean from this as far as the 5th commandment is concerned? Both Mary and Jesus' siblings at times boycotted our Lord's ministry. They clearly distanced themselves from him publicly. They had not learned yet to bear the reproach of acknowledging Christ as Lord and God. Despite those deep-seated failures, our Lord still honored and took care of His mother when she needed Him most. Perhaps, it would be wise to follow His example.

Practical Outworking of the 5th Commandment

We trained our children, after opting out of Social Security, to understand these truths concerning the 5th commandment and their obligation before God. According to God's design, parents are to take care of children when they are

young and children take care of parents as they age. Tragically, this Biblical model for family has been somewhat discarded in our day. In fact, I would dare say that much of our
government's welfare programs have been established to replace God's design for families.

As parents age, there may be times when the medical ne-
cessity is so great that they must be placed in nursing homes.
Keep in mind, however, that many of our aging parents suffer
impersonal care as a result. Many are reduced to a number,
while the remaining members of the family are minimally
involved or forsake their parents entirely. This is a grievous
betrayal of family in the eyes of God.

Other Challenges

There will be other challenges to negotiate as you seek
to establish honor in your home. Children are influenced by
the media, entertainment, modern technology, dreaded peer
pressure and a whole host of other outside sources. These
other entities carry some significance in their lives. God requires children, however, to place more weight on the influence of godly parents than all the other sources combined.

On a personal note, most of our children had no problem
honoring me as father. They thought they had options, however, when it came to their mother, especially, as my sons got
older. They somewhat resented being bossed by a woman.
Parents need to negotiate through that process as sons transition from boys to men. To a certain degree, they must cut
the skirt strings to develop as men. They must do so, however, without dishonoring their mom.

My first wife, who passed away, and my second bride were
and are Proverbs 31, Titus 2 women of God. Both were and
are soft spoken women. My children, at times, confused their
meekness for weakness. I had to straighten out that notion
by warning my children, "When mom whispers, hear dad's

thunder." If they do not honor mom, they do not honor dad and if they do not honor their parents, they do not honor God.

As children age, our relationship as parents change with them. The honor system must change as well. We go from being commanders to advisors as they mature. Once they are married, this reality becomes fully established.

It can be as difficult transition for both parent and children, but a necessary one. We must be careful how we handle this passing of the baton and our children establishing their own distinct families apart from their parents. Far too many parents interfere with their children's marriages with disastrous results.

As Christians, we should adopt the "leave and cleave" policy instituted by the Lord (Genesis 2:24). Only in cases of emergency should parents interject themselves in the marriage of their children. If our children solicit advice, we stand ready to give godly counsel. Otherwise, avoid being a busy body and interfere with their affairs.

Chapter Eight:
Family Lessons, Part One

These last two chapters will concentrate on a variety of family lessons that will prayerfully assist in raising godly children in a godless age. I asked my thirteen children what lessons, teachings, principles, and phrases had the most impact on their lives for good. The following is a compilation with no particular order.

Before these lessons are presented, however, I want to present a challenge. Hopefully, it will inspire you to press on to the high call and prize as parents. Let me briefly ask these questions. What are you living for as a couple and a family? Is it wealth, fame, education, prestige, reputation, security or something transcendent? What do you seek to accomplish before you shuffle off this mortal coil? What is the legacy and heritage you seek to leave as a family?

There are a few goals that I have chosen as a Christian man, husband, father, and minister of the Gospel of the Kingdom to fulfill in this vain, fleeting life. The first one should be a no brainer for any Christian worth their salt. In the Judgement, people will hear one of two statements from the Lord. It will be either: "Depart from Me, you cursed, into the everlasting fire prepared for the devil and his angels" or "Well done, good and faithful servant; you were faithful over a few things, I will make you ruler over many things. Enter into the joy of your Lord" (Matthew 25:41, 25:23) Wisdom and a healthy dose of self-preservation dictates the latter option.

Thus, my first recommendation is for you to live as a family to hear these words from our Lord, "Well done, thou good and faithful servants." I've seen some begin well in the race of faith but end badly. Avoid shipwreck and infidelity to the Lord and each other at all costs (1 Timothy 1:19).

Secondly, (and this goes above and beyond the call of duty) think about going the extra mile in service to our Lord. There have been children of God who achieved an incredible status worth emulating in Scripture. God's Word testifies that there were saints of old for whom "the world was not worthy" (Hebrews 11:32-40).

Before we meet the Lord face to face, would it not be glorious to be a part of that company? This will not be accomplished by casual, compromised, or a comfortable Americanized Christianity. A cross-less Christianity is a powerless Christianity. In other words, avoid being one who has a form of godliness, but denies its power (2 Timothy 3:5).

We must remember that this life is not a dress rehearsal. We do not get to perform do overs. Reincarnation is a delusion. We have one opportunity to run this race of faith, fight the battle, do the work, obey God's will, and give our best to advance Christ's Kingdom in the earth. Let's do this with the peace of God ruling our hearts, His joy being our strength, and His love consuming our souls.

Lastly, as we point our children to Christ for the salvation of their souls, it is inevitable that we must decrease as God must increase in their lives (John 3:30). Our goal as parents is to have our children "be in subjection to the Father of spirits and live" (Hebrews 12:9).

It is crucial that the impact of this transition be not a complete shock to their moral and spiritual sensibilities. While teaching Christ is important, it is modeling Christ that seals the deal for most children. As we fade, and Christ appears, let us make sure that He does not appear as a stranger to our children. To have some of God's goodness, love, and truth operating in our lives as parents will help greatly in this much needed transition. These are good and worthy goals to achieve as a family. Let us now proceed to other valuable truths and lessons.

Modern Technology and Your Children

We know many Christian couples who have gone the extra mile to protect their children from this godless age. The one thing that blindsided most of them was the advent of modern technology, social media and a world addicted to screens. Most of this generation seems to have been born adept to this wireless generation. They come out of the womb able to handle the state-of-the-art gadgets much better than their parents. This puts parents at a major disadvantage when it comes to what impacts their children.

If my wife and I had known better, we would have been much more circumspect before connecting our children to the internet. We were not aware of all the dangers. Though, we were prepared to protect them from the hazardous side of reality, we were not fully equipped to guide them through the perils of virtual reality. There were hosts of threats, such as, chat rooms, unsavory websites, and children communicating through the night with other youths unsupervised.

Some of our children have been hurt by this, but praise be to God, the Lord recovered them from the snare of the Evil One. As a result of not knowing how the enemy of our souls is gaining access to our children's minds through the internet, many families are suffering loss and damage. Make sure your family does not become a casualty.

On the one hand, it is hard to avoid the grid. It carries the future. It is no longer just weapons that control power amongst nations, but information that can be weaponized. This is causing an economic shift in how we do business. To a certain degree, we must train our children how to be savvy with these new developments, without them being beguiled by them.

If you are going to connect your children to the World Wide Web, take precautions. Much of the American mind has been fragmented by these technological advancements. It is producing a media-consumed generation addicted to fast-paced action. Too many of our young are preoccupied with short bursts of stimulating images.

What is the downside to these amusements? They limit children's attention span, desensitizes them to evil, and creates overweight, passive, coach potatoes who find it increasingly difficult to function in reality. Virtual reality and the drugs we give them to focus have captivated them. Modern technology gives them a sense of accomplishment without actual achievement.

On the other hand, this modern technology can be the church's new "Roman Road." "All roads lead to Rome" is a historical statement. Rome's conquest of much of the known world required massive road construction. These roads provided the necessary pathway for Rome's legions, weaponry, and pageantry to spread their empire.

In God's providence, those same roads became the pathway to spread the Gospel of the Kingdom. The Apostle Paul testified that the Christian faith had traversed the entire known world conquered by Rome in his life time (Romans 1:8; Colossians 1:3-6). Those roads were instrumental to the advancement of God's Kingdom during the early church's tremendous expansion.

At a click of a mouse not only can we and our children be subjected to porn and other harmful websites, but we can also use the same click of a mouse to reach multitudes with the truth and love of Christ. Therefore, it would be prudent to take the time to train your children to use this technology wisely. It can be a useful tool in life, but it must not replace our lives. With all due diligence, make sure you cut off all access routes to pornography.

Self-Government, the Key to Liberty

Taking a cue from our Founding Fathers, the Thomas Nation (The name we designated for our family) incorporated this principle as a primary training strategy. As kids get older, they obviously long for more flexibility and freedom. Of course, they still need supervision as they navigate to adulthood. If they can monitor themselves and exercise self-government, the process becomes easier.

Here is the principle: If our children maintained their integrity, they achieved a measure of freedom. If at any time they failed, we pulled back the reins to provide more supervision. This quote was a constant reminder in training our children. It comes from Robert Winthrop. He stated, "Men, in a word, must necessarily be controlled, either by a power within them, or by a power without them; either by the Word of God, or by the strong arm of man; either by the Bible, or by the bayonet." Only a spiritually fit and moral people are capable to handle freedom properly. This is not only true for nations, it is also true for raising godly children in a godless age.

Many children long for the benefits of adulthood but fail at the responsibilities that come with it. They must learn that they cannot have one without the other. Self-government, which leads to liberty helps families negotiate through the awkward stage that spans from childhood to adulthood.

Delegated Authority

One of the major advantages of having a large family besides fulfilling Psalms 127:3-5, obeying the cultural, dominion mandate (Genesis 1:26-28), and filling the world with godly seed (Malachi 2:15), are the powerful Biblical lessons to be learned. One of them that is crucial to children's maturity is understanding the principle of delegated authority.

Most of this generation has grown up in a fatherless and

lawless culture. Properly relating to God ordained authorities has not been their strong suit. For many, the answer to tyranny is anarchy. We see this mentality displayed throughout the land.

The Scriptures teach that Jesus marveled on two occasions. Once was at the unbelief of Jews who should have known better and the other concerned a despised Roman Centurion that exercised great faith in our Lord (Mark 6:5, 6; Matthew 8:5-13). It seems this Roman Centurion recognized our Lord as the Supreme Authority. He also had a good grasp concerning the concept of delegated authority (Romans 13:1-4).

When pleading for the life of his servant who was dear to him, the Roman Centurion knew that the Jews were banned from entering the home of a "Gentile dog." This prohibition did not cause our Lord to hesitate in the least. Jesus was willing to break with tradition to come heal his servant. The Roman, however, interjected, "Lord, I am not worthy that You should come under my roof. But only speak a word, and my servant will be healed. For I also am a man under authority, having soldiers under me. And I say to this one, 'Go,' and he goes; and to another, 'Come,' and he comes; and to my servant, 'Do this,' and he does it" (Matthew 8;8, 9). The Roman Centurion connected faith with delegated authority and received his heart felt request miraculously.

How these truths break down within the family is key to a child's development. When older siblings are responsible enough to watch younger children, it's time to introduce this concept. Parents should diligently instruct older siblings to rule justly in their stead (2 Samuel 23:3).

The training includes a spiritual diagnostic test to first reveal their heart condition. Respect for elders and genuine care for youngsters are mandatory. No rolling of the eyes. No passive rebellion. No talking back. True honor for those older and a compassionate concern for youngers is obligatory.

As older siblings develop these virtues, they should be trained to know the parent's standards for the home. It is their duty to simply reinforce them when parents are not present. Physical and spiritual safety are the desired goals for all concerned, including the older siblings.

Older ones are not to abuse their delegated authority. They are not to play the tyrant and give unlawful orders to their younger siblings. The "Golden Rule" must be applied even when establishing the concept of delegated authority. How you want to be treated when you are the delegated authority is how you treat those under your delegated authority.

Parents must also instruct the younger siblings how to submit to this Biblical principle. The youngers are to obey all lawful instructions. They are not, however, obligated to obey unlawful orders. If older siblings entice them to sin, the younger siblings must obey God, rather than man (Acts 5:29). In our age of governmental tyranny and cultural anarchy, this precept is a must in training our children to be faithful to the Lord.

It would be good to set in the delegated authority before the whole family. All parties need to know the parent's expectations. If the older siblings are speaking the same thing as their parents and following the parent's instructions, obedience is required by the younger siblings. If the younger children disobey, they are not just defying the delegated authority. They are defying the parent's authority, which ultimately defies God's authority.

The younger siblings need to be encouraged that the time will come when they will be called upon to be the delegated authority. So, how they obey lawful instructions will determine their capacity to issue future directives. The concept is simple. How you receive instruction will have a direct impact upon your integrity to give instructions.

In other words, they will not always be the follower. The time will come when they will be the leader. How do they want followers to respond to their leadership when it comes to being set in as the delegated authority? It starts by being a good follower.

This precept is also a great way to train children in good parenting skills. Most kids today are clueless when it comes to this crucial preparation for life. We taught our kids from a young age on the true measure of success. It is not measured by wealth, fame, education or social status. It is measured by fulfilling the major roles that our Creator has established for the human race. They are son/daughter, brother/sister, husband/wife, father/mother, and if you live long enough, grandfather/grandmother.

What if we gain the whole world and become abject failures where it counts most in life (Mark 8:36)? We can accumulate much in this world, but if we cannot rest it on a solid foundation of faith and family, what have we accomplished that is of eternal value?

Spend your time wisely training children to be successful sons and daughters, brothers and sisters. Develop them to become successful husbands and wives. Mature them to become successful fathers and mothers. This way whatever else they may gain in this world will rest on a solid foundation, which will lead to greater blessings in their lives.

Proverbs promises, "The blessing of the Lord makes one rich, and He adds no sorrow with it" (Proverbs 10:22). Pursuing riches may gain wealth but if we are not careful, we can lose what is most important in life. The blessing can become a curse.

The Scriptures warn:

But those who desire to be rich fall into temptation and a snare, and into many foolish and harmful lusts which drown men in destruction and perdition. For

94

the love of money is a root of all kinds of evil, for which
some have strayed from the faith in their greediness,
and pierced themselves through with many sorrows
(1 Timothy 6:9, 10).

Make sure your family's priority system avoids this travesty by developing a godly value system.

Family Reading Times

Besides reading through the Bible each year at our family
altar, one of our family practices that proved beneficial for
our children was our family reading times at night. It is good
to turn the TV off on occasions and just spend time together
as a family. We purposely tried to instill in our children a
love for reading and learning. Readers are leaders. We as-
signed them books primarily centered on theology, history,
and biographies.

Our children grew up studying great men and women of
faith. They grew to admire the courage of those who have
gone before us whom God used to touch nations and change
the world. They thrilled to hear the great exploits of mission-
aries and the dangers they endured for the cause of Christ.

We trained our boys to be strong of limb, keen of wit, and
fervent of spirit. We used the King David model to inspire
our sons to become poets, (Develop a romantic, artistic soul)
warriors, (Endure hardness as a good soldier of Jesus Christ)
and statesmen (Think and act governmentally, jurisdictionally, and principally).

Being raised to minister at death camps (Abortion mills)
they learned the "no greater love" ethic taught by our Lord.
They were instructed to employ their manhood to protect
and care for women and children. (John 15:13). Inspirational
true stories like the Scottish troop transport ship, the Birken-
head, and later the example set by the sacrificial men aboard

95

the Titanic helped develop these godly manhood traits in their lives.

Both sons and daughters were admonished to be gentle-men and ladies. Their duty was to care for the unpopular, befriend the outcast, avoid popularity cliques, and stick up for the little guy being bullied. They were taught when you go somewhere do not seek to be the center of attention, but look for those less fortunate to minister, love, and serve. Did they do it perfectly? Not by a long shot, but they did bear some good Kingdom fruit pursuing these virtues.

Work Ethic

Human beings tend to be lazy by nature. This generation has taken that vice and perfected it to an art form. Millen-nials are known as the "entitlement generation" and hell has no fury like telling Millennials no. The word "no" is a foreign concept to many of them as it may hurt their "inner child." It has deteriorated to the point that college age students need "safe zones" to protect them from opinions that may be con-trary to their fragile worldview.

Couple that with participation trophies and America has produced a "bubble wrapped generation" that is ill prepared to handle the rigors of life. Rewarding laziness, catering to sloth, indulging, pampering, and coddling young adults is a national travesty with far reaching consequences.

The second law of thermodynamics teaches that there is a natural predisposition of any isolated system to decline into a chaotic state. There were times when discussing this natural state, I would ask my children, "What would happen to our yard, if we did not expend the energy to keep it mowed?" They instinctively knew it would become unmanageable. It would be overgrown with weeds, thorns, and thistles. So, it is with life. It takes effort, diligence, and perseverance to over-come the natural state of affairs to be organized and product-tive.

As Christians birthed into God's Kingdom, we should desire and work to better life. Not only for ourselves, but for others (Philippians 2:4). It is a part of the cultural mandate instituted by God (Genesis 1:28). Work was not a part of the curse upon man. Adam had been given instructions to tend and keep the garden (Genesis 2:15). All the curse did was make sure our work would be accompanied by the sweat of our brow. Instead of God's creation yielding to the touch of men, there would now be resistance associated with our work that men would have to overcome to enjoy the fruit of their labor.

Despite the Fall, the cultural mandate command has never been rescinded. One of the main reasons why America exploded as an economic power house at our founding was due to the Protestant, Evangelical work ethic our ancestors derived from this Biblical mandate.

It is good to take what we have found in life and transform it by God's grace and power. We should leave something finer than the way we discovered it. We sought to instill this value system in our offspring.

Considering these truths, we raised our children to be "Salmon" Christians. Everything dead in a river just flows with the current. God forbid our children walk in lockstep with the spirit of the age. Our children need to be raised to go against the status quo of this fallen world and their own inclination towards laziness. They need to head upstream, which requires due diligence.

In pursuing this course, we encouraged our children to be orange Christians rather than apple Christians. What is the difference? An apple has thin skin and a hard inside. The orange has tough skin and a soft inside. Working hard, doing your best, and going the extra mile is demanding. There will be bumps and bruises along the way. We need to make sure

97

our children have a tough exterior to handle pressure and stress, while maintaining soft hearts and tender consciences as they make their way through life.

Here is what Proverbs teaches on this important topic. This is just a portion addressing laziness and contrasting that with diligence.

"He who has a slack hand becomes poor, but the hand of the diligent makes rich" (Proverbs 10:4).

"The hand of the diligent will rule, but the lazy man will be put to forced labor" (Proverbs 12:24).

"The lazy man will not plow because of winter; He will beg during harvest and have nothing" (Proverbs 20:4).

"I went by the field of the lazy man, and by the vineyard of the man devoid of understanding; and there it was, all overgrown with thorns; Its surface was covered with nettles; Its stone wall was broken down. When I saw it, I considered it well; I looked on it and received instruction: A little sleep, a little slumber, a little folding of the hands to rest; so shall your poverty come like a prowler, and your need like an armed man" (Proverbs 24:30-34).

"The lazy man says, "There is a lion in the road! A fierce lion is in the streets" (Proverbs 26:13)!

"Do you see a man who excels in his work? He will stand before kings; He will not stand before unknown men" (Proverbs 22:29).

There is more to gain from Proverbs warnings against laziness and its encouragement to embrace diligence. This will suffice for now. Keep in mind, however, that our Lord was not sheepish in denouncing laziness. Matthew 25:26 states, "But his lord answered and said to him, 'You wicked and lazy servant, you knew that I reap where I have not sown, and gather where I have not scattered seed.'" As you can see, it never ends well for the lazy, both here and now and the age to come.

Unfortunately, our nation uses welfare in many cases to subsidize slothful behavior. This practically ensures no one will gain wisdom to reject the folly of laziness and find the incentive to better their lives. Regardless, no one in their right minds should want their children to become a slave to laziness, government handouts, and the dreadful consequences that will follow in its wake. Instilling a strong work ethic in our children is the cure to overcome these snares.

Focusing on the task at hand is one of the keys to training children to overcome the natural propensity towards laziness. Concentration to detail and following through to completion is the worthy objective. As parents, we did not want to micromanage every single detail of assignments given to our children. We encouraged them to be faithful to avoid us looking over their shoulder. How could they accomplish this? They needed to do the job right the first time by going above and beyond the call of duty.

This was a little poem by an unknown author we had our children memorize. It captured our philosophy on training our children to have a strong work ethic.

Work while you work, play while you play; one thing each time that is the way. All that you do, do with all you're might; Things done by half are not done right.

"Wherever you are at, be all there" remains our constant motto.

The desired result we taught our children in pursuing a strong work ethic was to make themselves indispensable. If hired for a job, they should want the boss to make an investment to keep them. Good character, promptness, paying attention to instruction, and diligence to get the job done right the first time would certainly help achieve that righteous goal. The boss should miss them, if they ever had to leave to pursue God's will for their futures.

Chapter Nine:
Family Lessons, Part 2

O God, You have taught me from my youth; And to this day I declare Your wondrous works. Now also when I am old and grayheaded, O God, do not forsake me, Until I declare Your strength to this generation, Your power to everyone who is to come (Psalms 71:17, 18).

To raise godly children in a godless age requires a multi-generational vision. In a relay race, no matter how swift the runners, it is the passing of the baton that determines victory or defeat in the race of life. Training children in the concept of the continuum is essential in passing the Kingdom baton successfully to the next generation

It is revealed in Psalms 71 that King David had a multi-generational vision and mission. This poet, warrior, states-man was keenly aware of life's continuum—the past, the present, and the future. Notice first, he acknowledged the training received from his youth. What was the nature of his instructions? It is safe to assume that he learned the history of his people and God's dealings with Israel. At an early age, David discovered his glorious legacy and righteous heritage. He also learned of Israel's many failings and God's warnings to his people. This knowledge was essential to frame his vi-sionary leadership.

Not content to remain in the bygone era, King David ap-plied the lessons from Israel's past to his present time. He prayed to demonstrate God's strength to his generation. As he matured in years and in faith, however, his commitment to God extended to future generations.

He longed to influence a people who were not yet born. King David wanted God to impact his posterity, even though they would never meet him on this side of eternity. Did God honor his request and fulfill his understanding of the continuum? Judge for yourself; Acts 13:36 states, "For David, after he had served his own generation by the will of God, fell on sleep, and was laid unto his fathers, and saw corruption."

In our homeschool, the University of Righteousness, we constructed a historical timeline to teach our children the powerful lessons of the continuum. Historical events, key leaders, and God's intervention in time and history fill our walls. At the end of the timeline, we placed a picture of each family member. For those who are aged or are now with the Lord, we added a brief explanation as to their individual contribution to "His story." This is to instill in our children a sense of God's destiny and to demonstrate that they have come into God's kingdom "for such a time as this" (Esther 4:14).

I cannot emphasize enough how important these lessons are in raising godly children in a godless age. Most young people cannot see the forest from the trees. Their perspective is limited by their generation. It is critical our children study history, know their heritage, learn from the past, apply time honored truths to the present and then live their lives to impact the future for God's Kingdom and glory.

There was another king in Israel. At times, he was considered a good king. He is one, however, who failed to pass on a multi-generational vision to his children. He dropped the baton and did not seem to care what that might mean to his posterity.

If you recall, King Hezekiah came down with a life-threatening illness. Isaiah, the prophet, told him to get his affairs in order before he died. Hezekiah upon hearing this news sought the Lord to grant him a reprieve. The Lord mercifully answered his cry and granted 15 more years to his life.

They were not good years. He gave birth to one of the most wicked kings in Israel's turbulent history. King Manasseh,

Hezekiah's son, filled Jerusalem with innocent blood and established abject idolatry in Israel (2 Kings 21).

Afterwards, when Babylon sent envoys to Hezekiah to spy out his house of treasures, Hezekiah proudly complied with all their wishes. It was a major lapse in judgment. When Isaiah found out, he enquired of Hezekiah if the report was true. Hezekiah responded in the affirmative. Isaiah warned:

> Hear the word of the LORD: Behold, the days are coming when all that is in your house, and what your fathers have accumulated until this day, shall be carried to Babylon; nothing shall be left,' says the LORD. 'And they shall take away some of your sons who will descend from you, whom you will beget; and they shall be eunuchs in the palace of the king of Babylon'" (2 Kings 20:16-18).

How did Hezekiah respond to this disturbing news? It was a sad commentary on his notion of fatherhood. He stated, "The word of the LORD which you have spoken is good!" For he said, "Will there not be peace and truth at least in my days" (2 Kings 20:19)? What is missing from his response? There seems to be no care or acknowledgement of what will befall his children's future based upon his folly.

Tragically, far too many in my generation seem to have adopted the Hezekiah model rather than the King David model when it comes to passing a multi-generational vision to their children. Make sure your family chooses the latter and eschew the former. While you are at, encourage other families to do likewise.

Wisdom, Knowledge, and Understanding

The LORD by wisdom founded the earth; By understanding He established the heavens; By His knowledge the depths were broken up, and clouds drop down the dew (Proverbs 3:19, 20).

Since the Lord utilized wisdom, understanding, and knowledge to create the heavens and earth, we always thought these virtues would be essential to raise godly children in a godless age. Thankfully, the Lord in His great benevolence also made these godly attributes available to his fallen creatures. They are essential for great works of art, craftsmanship, and statesmanship.

When Moses was tapped to build the tabernacle of the Lord, he had to make sure he crafted it down to the finest detail. This was no small task. Thankfully, God raised up a paraclete to come along side of Moses to make sure the job was completed according to God's specific designs. The man's name was Bezalel the son of Uri, the son of Hur, from the tribe of Judah.

Notice how the Lord equipped this man for this sacred task, "And I have filled him with the Spirit of God, in wisdom, in understanding, in knowledge, and in all manner of workmanship, to design artistic works, to work in gold, in silver, in bronze, in cutting jewels for setting, in carving wood, and to work in all manner of workmanship" (Exodus 31:3-5).

The same attributes God used to create the heavens and earth are the same qualities exercised by Bezalel to build the tabernacle. It is no small task to instill these godly characteristics in the life of our children. To do so properly, definition of terms is required.

Some say knowledge is power. There are those, however, who according to the Scripture gain incredible knowledge but become educated fools in the process. When God calls people fools, He is not critiquing their level of intellect. He is judging their presuppositions that lead to a lapse of moral character (Psalms 14:1). 2 Timothy 3:7 teaches that humans

103

can be very studious and end up, "always learning and never able to come to the knowledge of the truth."

Our colleges are filled, both professors and students, with this betrayal against sound learning. Knowledge that does not lead to truth, critical thinking, and godly character misses the mark. Think twice before considering sending your children to college. Typically, that is where and when the enemy of our souls swoops down and captures our arrows. Instead of our children being shot from the bow of family and church to take Satan out, he captures them to take our families out. Avoid this intellectual and spiritual treachery at all costs.

Knowledge is the gaining of data, statistics, and information. The capacity of the brain to absorb knowledge is phenomenal, especially, in the modern era. We have an overload of knowledge flooding our brains at a rapid pace. According to Jeff Shultz from Big Data Zone:

> If we do some quick calculations, we can see the amount of data created on the internet each day. There are 1,440 minutes per day... so that means that there are approximately:
>
> • 1,209,600 new data-producing social media users each day.
> • 656 million tweets per day!
> • More than four million hours of content uploaded to YouTube every day, with users watching 5.97 billion hours of YouTube videos each day.
> • 67,305,600 Instagram posts uploaded each day,
> • There are over two billion monthly active Facebook users, compared to 1.44 billion at the start of 2015 and 1.65 at the start of 2016.
> • Facebook has 1.32 billion daily active users on average as of June 2017.

- 4.3 billion Facebook messages posted daily!
- 5.75 billion Facebook likes every day.
- 22 billion texts sent every day.
- 5.2 billion daily Google Searches in 2017.

That is a lot of knowledgeable information available to discern and absorb. The problem with gaining knowledge on a massive scale is ignorance of the moral component. Not all knowledge is good. In fact, some knowledge like the tree of the knowledge of good and evil can prove fatal (Genesis 2:17). Since the Fall, man has had unlawful desires to know the future, manipulate outcomes, and determine results. False prophets seduce people with "hidden knowledge" to reinforce the bondage of the Fall, which is to be a law and god unto ourselves.

The early church had great battles against the Gnostics to protect God's people from their heretical pursuit of "hidden knowledge." Gnostics claimed "to know" higher truths that were only available to the intellectual elite. This knowledge came not from the Bible but from a higher mystical plane of consciousness. Couple that with the gnostic assertion that matter is inherently evil, and spirit is good and you have a recipe for theological and doctrinal disasters. As a result of these presuppositions, Gnostics believe anything done in the body, even what God considers abominations, has no real meaning. According to Gnostics, real life exists in the spirit realm only.

In the midst of these and other seductive deceptions, the prophet Isaiah declared:

And when they say to you, "Seek those who are mediums and wizards, who whisper and mutter," should not a people seek their God? Should they seek the dead on behalf of the living? To the law and to the testimony! If they do not speak according to this word,

105

it is because there is no light in them (Isaiah 8:19, 20).

Knowledge is foundational to growth, development, and maturity. By itself, it lacks the temperance to guard the mind from error, deception, and faulty logic. The Apostle Paul warned, "Beware lest anyone cheat you through philosophy and empty deceit, according to the tradition of men, according to the basic principles of the world, and not according to Christ" (Colossians 2:8).

The love for wisdom, the pursuit of the study of the nature of knowledge, and the quest to gain the meaning of life is what drives the philosophical impulse in man. If this pursuit is not rooted and grounded in Christ, it will betray us from ever obtaining these noble aspirations. It is in Christ alone where we can safely discover "all the treasures of wisdom and knowledge" (Colossians 2:3).

There is something else required to temper the pursuit of knowledge that is essential to promote soundness of mind within our children (2 Timothy 1:7). It is called understanding. Proverbs teaches, "The fear of the Lord is the beginning of wisdom, and the knowledge of the Holy One is understanding" (Proverbs 9:10). Knowing the Holy One and what He considers holy is the basis for proper understanding.

Understanding is God's umpire to judge knowledge. Just like a baseball umpire determines balls or strikes, understanding determines the difference between lawful knowledge that is good to keep and evil knowledge that is to be rejected. God wants us wise to what is good and simple when it comes to evil (Romans 16:19).

In one of our Lord's parables concerning the Kingdom, we discern the purpose for understanding. Matthew 13:47, 48 teaches, "Again, the kingdom of heaven is like a dragnet that was cast into the sea and gathered some of every kind, which, when it was full, they drew to shore; and they sat

106

down and gathered the good into vessels, but threw the bad away." This parable not only reveals truths concerning God's Kingdom, but also discloses the function of understanding. Understanding is key to discern the true nature of knowledge.

This leads to the critical importance of wisdom. Wisdom is the proper application of knowledge and understanding. This is key. One can obtain sound knowledge and proper understanding, but without applying it, what good are these other godly attributes? It is like "faith without works is dead" syndrome (James 2:26).

Wisdom takes knowledge and understanding to guide our decision-making capabilities. It serves in many ways to make the complex simple. Through the fog of moral dilemmas, pressurized situations, and stressful circumstances, wisdom stands ready to lead and guide.

Whereas the New Testament promotes love as the highest virtue to obtain, the Old Testament prizes wisdom (1 Corinthians 13:13; Proverbs 4:7). Proverbs teaches that wisdom is the principle thing. It is important for us and our children to not only obtain wisdom, we must also ensure we retain it.

Solomon, the author of Proverbs, was blessed with a divine encounter with God to obtain wisdom (1 Kings 3:4-14). His wisdom was world renowned. He astonished Israel and was the envy of heads of state (1 Kings 3:16-28; 1 Kings 4:30, 34). In his life, he tallied about 3000 wise maxims (1 Kings 4:32). Tragically, he also married many foreign women. He continually violated God's standards for kings. He plunged Israel into idolatry, which betrayed God's wisdom in his life (1 Kings 11:1-4; Deuteronomy 17:14-20; 1 Kings 4:26). As much as lies within you, make sure this does not befall you or your children.

A good way to ensure your children keep the wisdom they obtain is by looking to the book of James. Clearly, the

Apostle James drew heavily from the book of Proverbs in penning his epistle. His language, precepts, and directives matched it greatly. His additional contribution distinguishes between the wisdom of the world and the wisdom that comes from God. He describes the wisdom of the world as "earthly, sensual, demonic" (James 3:15b). The fruits of this kind of wisdom produce envy, self-seeking, confusion and every evil thing (James 3:16).

In contrast, is the wisdom that comes from God that He will grant with the asking (James 1:5). James describes heavenly wisdom in these terms, "But the wisdom that is from above is first pure, then peaceable, gentle, willing to yield, full of mercy and good fruits, without partiality and without hypocrisy. Now the fruit of righteousness is sown in peace by those who make peace" (James 3:17, 18). To ensure peace in your home, training your children to exercise godly wisdom is paramount.

Stewardship

Moreover it is required in stewards that one be found faithful (1 Corinthians 4:2).

If I said it once, I said it a thousand times, "Treat things according to design." The light fan is not built to act as an amusement park ride nor a barber's blade to cut hair. I'll leave that to your imagination as to what that might mean in our household.

Our Lord is the glorious Designer. He established fixed laws in the universe to operate consistently. Without the laws of physics, science would not be possible nor the advancement of technology. If the conditions of the universe evolved or fluctuated on a continual basis, no experimentation could reach a conclusive discovery. Christian scientists of old believed they were blessed to think God's thoughts after Him.

God's moral laws point true north. They are extensions of

his righteous, holy, and just character. They are also fixed. The Lord changes not. On the moral front, there are reasons why the homosexual agenda causes so much damage to individuals who practice this abomination and our nation, which condones it.

One of them is not treating the human body according to design. Therefore, their sexuality is labeled unnatural. The natural use has been abandoned and something that is contrary to nature has replaced it. Two male parts and two female parts together does not produce the spark of life.

The result is a breakdown of the human body, mind, and spirit. Most homosexuals reduce their life span in half by practicing this deviant lifestyle. God will not be mocked. What a man sows that shall he also reap. If we sow to the flesh, we reap corruption. If we sow to the Spirit, everlasting life and peace is the blessed fruit (Galatians 6:7, 8). Only the glorious Gospel can set homosexuals free and restore them back to the natural use.

Treating things according to design drives home the importance of being good stewards. When God grants us spiritual and/or material gifts, we should take care of His blessings. Inculcating this Biblical concept is just another key to fulfill our stated goals.

Renewing our minds with the Word of God, caring of our bodies through personal hygiene, maintaining our health by exercise, proper diet, and rest, and taking care of our possessions are beneficial practices promoting sound stewardship.

Jesus taught:

> He who is faithful in what is least is faithful also in much; and he who is unjust in what is least is unjust also in much. Therefore if you have not been faithful in the unrighteous mammon, who will commit to your trust the true riches? And if you have not been

faithful in what is another man's, who will give you
what is your own (Luke 16:10-12)?

We emphasized this teaching to help our children exercise good stewardship. Being faithful in the little things pre-
pares our children to receive God's promotions. Taking care
of business at home leads them to take care of business later.

Children need to know that if our Christianity is not
working at home, it diminishes our public witness. We should
not try to export globally, what is not working locally. Our
foundations must be firm at home to build properly abroad
(1 Corinthians 3:10).

Family is the launching pad for effective public ministry.
A man's credibility as a Christian leader is judged by the behavior of his family. The Apostle Paul reminds us in I Timothy 3:4, 5, "One who rules his own house well, having his
children in submission with all reverence (for if a man does
not know how to rule his own house, how will he take care of
the church of God?)" The lesson is clear. If a man cannot take
care of his bride and family, God does not want that man to
take care of His bride and family.

Each child is an important link in the chain of effectual
service to God as a family. The chain is only as strong as the
weakest link. Impress these truths upon their souls. The entire family needs to take ownership for the faith once and for
all delivered to the saints and its implications in the earth
(Jude 1:3).

We taught our children to walk in integrity as good stewards of God's favor in their lives. They were trained to look
adults in the eye, give a hearty hand shake, and converse
properly with respect. Their word must be their bond. They
should keep their word, even if they suffer harm in the process. Short term, they may experience loss, but long term, it
will greatly benefit them.

Proverbs reveals, "A good name is to be chosen rather than great riches, loving favor rather than silver and gold (Proverbs 22:1). Passing your children a good family name (warts and all) and your encouragement to maintain that good name is a heritage worth pursuing. It is part of employing good stewardship goals.

Additionally, we encouraged our children to be good stewards of God's favor by achieving greatness. Not by the world's standards, but the Lord's standards. Being servant of all is one of the benchmarks for achieving Biblical greatness (Matthew 20:26). The other Biblical measure for greatness according to Jesus was teaching and obeying His commandments (Matthew 5:19). It is this greatness that we desired our children to accomplish as good stewards.

Establishing consistency in these matters cuts down on the natural tendency for our children to play the hypocrite. If you recall, Greek theatre used masks to identify role changes. One person could play several roles by merely switching masks. This is where the idea of playing the hypocrite emerged.

The challenge to children is for them to be the same person whether parents are watching them or not. Giving eye-service as a man pleaser should be frowned upon. Doing the will of God from the heart is what should be expected (Ephesians 6:6, 7).

What people do in private reveals to a certain extent the true mettle of their character. Our private and public life should mesh. A bad tree cannot produce good fruit (Matthew 7:18). If children adapt to their environment and change like a chameleon something is fractured in their souls. There is a mental and moral disconnect, if they keep changing masks to be accepted by their peers.

Establishing loyalty to God, His Word, and God-ordained relationships leads to good stewardship skills. Moreover, be

111

more concerned about children exercising self-control rather than self-esteem secures the quality of faithfulness the Lord requires as stewards.

Gifts of God are given. We do not earn them. We have the solemn responsibility, however, to be good stewards of them. We can fail or betray God's gifts, but we will still be held accountable. The gifts and callings of God are without repentance (Romans 11:29). Godly fruit, however, is grown. Faithful plowing, sowing, and watering paves the way for God to grant increase and produce a harvest in raising godly children in a godless age (1 Corinthians 3:6-8).

Last Admonition

And He said to them, "Come aside by yourselves to a deserted place and rest a while." For there were many coming and going, and they did not even have time to eat" (Mark 6:31).

As stated in the beginning of this book, raising godly children in a godless age is not for the faint at heart. It takes a consecrated effort. It demands a conscious dedication to stay faithful to this noble ambition. You will have to sacrifice, pay extra, and work harder than most parents in this modern age are willing to do to make this dream become a reality.

Your efforts, however, are not without notice from heaven and the Lord's rewards. God promised, "For God is not unjust to forget your work and labor of love which you have shown toward His name, in that you have ministered to the saints, and do minister" (Hebrews 6:10).

When the going gets tough as it tends to do, keep your eye on the prize. You shall reap, if you faint not (Galatians 6:9). Make sure in training your children that you unplug at times. Come aside by yourselves and rest. Take some time to enjoy some fun and family recreation. Create good memories.

Through the good, bad, and ugly that this life comprises,

one thing should rise above it all. It should come when you sit down with your family at the dinner table. As you pause to give thanks, take a good long, hard look at your children and grandchildren about you. Who knows, it may be at those precious times when waves of well-being may crash over your soul. A smile may appear and a thought radiate in your head, "It's **all been worth it.**" Yes, attempting to raise godly children in a godless age is worth every bit of it!

Rusty Lee Thomas was born in Cherry Point, NC on a Marine Base. He was raised on the mean streets of Bridgeport CT. At the age of sixteen, his parents divorced, he quit school, left home to live on his own, and most importantly, he came to the saving grace and knowledge of our Lord and Savior, Jesus Christ.

Rev. Rusty Lee Thomas   At the age of 17, Thomas joined the Army. He served as a M60-machine gunner with the 101st Airborne Division.

In his early twenties, God called him to leave Hollywood where he was pursuing an acting career and to go into full-time ministry. Since that time till now, Thomas has dedicated his life to serving His King and advancing His Kingdom in the earth.

Rev. Thomas has a father's mantle and spreads a patriarchal vision to reclaim the masculine identity that has been neutered by the feminization of America. He and his wife, Kendra Thomas, home schooled thirteen children at the Thomas Nation's University of Righteousness.

Rev. Thomas spent six years as a traveling evangelist and two years as a pastor in St. Petersburg, Fl. In 1994, he became the assistant director of Operation Rescue/Operation Save America, under the leadership of Rev. Flip Benham, national director of Operation Rescue/Operation Save America. Altogether, he has close to 40 years of experience as a full time minister, public speaker, and writer.

He is currently the Director of Operation Rescue/Operation Save America.

Stone River Books   P.O. Box 20712
Waco, Texas 76702

Made in the USA
Monee, IL
23 February 2021